Edward Clements Bigmore, Charles William Henry Wyman

A Bibliography of Printing

T - Z Inclusive

Edward Clements Bigmore, Charles William Henry Wyman

A Bibliography of Printing
T - Z Inclusive

ISBN/EAN: 9783337251079

Printed in Europe, USA, Canada, Australia, Japan

Cover: Foto ©Thomas Meinert / pixelio.de

More available books at **www.hansebooks.com**

A

BIBLIOGRAPHY OF PRINTING

VOLUME III.

A

BIBLIOGRAPHY

OF

PRINTING

WITH

NOTES & ILLUSTRATIONS

COMPILED BY

E. C. BIGMORE AND C. W. H. WYMAN

T—Z INCLUSIVE

LONDON

BERNARD QUARITCH, 15 PICCADILLY

MDCCCLXXXVI

N the Preface to the Second Volume of this "Bibliography of Printing," reference was made to the causes which rendered necessary the issue of a Third volume.

The first portion of the matter appeared in the *Printing Times and Lithographer* as far back as January, 1876. The first volume of the reproduction in book form went to press in 1880, the second in 1884. What has been described as a long and laborious task, but one correspondingly necessary and useful in the interests of the literature of the art, is now brought to a close.

It is obvious that the method of publication and the alphabetical system of arrangement of this work must have precluded the citation of many works which, if the "Bibliography" had been only now issued as a whole, would have been included. This shortcoming is remedied by the record and review of new books given in the journal above mentioned, and to which the yearly index gives immediate reference. It will be found, however, that an endeavour has been made to obviate this disadvantage by bringing the later articles, such as "Typography" up to date.

It had, certainly, at one time been intended to continue the catalogue in the shape of a Supplement, but the wishes of subscribers, anxious to see the completion of a work so long in progress, prevailed, and for the same reason a mass of valuable matter relative to the publications and history of Printers' Societies has been for the present withheld.

The health of Mr. CHARLES WYMAN, to which reference was made in the preceding volume, has not yet been restored, but the collaborateurs already mentioned have continued their valuable and most kindly assistance.

Mr. JOHN SOUTHWARD, to whose services allusion was made in the prefaces of the first two volumes, has revised and collated the various proof-sheets, and from the commencement has written the principal annotations and biographies. Mr. WILLIAM BLADES, Mr. THEODOR GOEBEL, of Stuttgart; Mr. JOHN H. HESSELS, of Cambridge; Mr. LOUIS MOHR, of Strasbourg; Mr. THEO. L. DE VINNE, of New York, and Mr. VAN DER HAEGEN, of Ghent,—names of the highest eminence in this department of Bibliography,— have all rendered invaluable aid, and contributed most materially to the carrying out of an enterprise the results of which are now in the hands of the reader.

TABELLEN über Kupferstecher-Arbeit. 2te Aufl. Leipzig : 1807.

TABLEAU des libraires et des imprimeurs-jurés de l'Université de Paris au 1ᵉʳ Février, 1787. Paris : 1787. 4to.

TABLEAU des libraires, imprimeurs et édi-teurs de livres des principales villes de l'Europe. Paris : 1804. 12mo. pp. 92.

On the half-title are the words : État des libraires et imprimeurs de l'Europe.

TABLEAU généalogique et bibliographique des trois grandes familles d'imprimeurs libraires les plus célèbres (les Estienne, les Alde, les Elzevier). Lille : 1853. Folio.

TABLEAU généalogique et héraldique de la Famille Estienne, originaire de Provence, depuis l'an 1270 jusqu'en 1826, avec les armoiries de quelques maisons qui lui ont été alliées, tant par les hommes que par les femmes, de laquelle sont issus les savants illustres et typographes de ce nom. Paris : 1852. 1 leaf, folio.

Dedicated to Firmin Didot. (*See* STEPHENS, *ante.*)

TABLEAU de Typographie universelle de Poche et d'Ambulance. Paris : 1828.

A folio broadside.

TACQUINET (Léon). Artiste graveur en taille-douce de xixᵉ siècle. 8vo. 1876. pp. 240.

TADINIO (Placido). Ellogium equitis Io. Baptistæ Bodonii inscrip-tionum stylo dispositum. Parmæ : 1816. 4to. pp. ix.

An elegant specimen of the famous Bodoni Press.

TAEUBEL. (C. G.). Allgemeines theoretisch-praktisches Wörterbuch der Buchdruckerkunst und Schriftgiesserey, in welchem
alle bey der Ausübung derselben vorkommende, und in die
damit verwandten Künste, Wissenschaften und Gewerbe
einschlagende Kunstwörter, nach alphabet. Ordnung deutlich
und ausführlich erklärt werden. 2 vols. Vienna: 1805. 4to.
pp. viii. 152 and viii. 88, with plates and many tables.

The Appendix contains the Homo-
nyms (that is, words variously spelled,
but similarly pronounced) of the German
Language, the Technical Terms used
in Printing, Schemes of Imposition, a

List of obsolete German words, of
Abbreviations, &c., a Cantata in honour
of the Art of Printing, and Speeches to
be pronounced on the Reception of a
new member of the Profession.

——— Kleines Formatbuch zum Gebrauch für Schriftsetzer. Buch-
holz : 1786. 8vo.

——— Orthotypographisches Handbuch, oder Anleitung zur gründ-
lichen Kenntniss derjenigen Theile der Buchdruckerkunst,
welche allen Schriftstellern, Buchhändlern, besonders aber denen
Correctoren unentbehrlich sind. Nebst einem Anhange eines
typographischen Wörterbuches. Halle und Leipzig : 1785. 8vo.
pp. 383, portrait, and several leaves of folding tables, &c.

——— Praktisches Handbuch der Buchdruckerkunst für Anfänger.
Two parts. Leipzig : 1791. 8vo. pp. viii. 228, folding-plates
of specimens.—Zweyter Theil. Typographisches Wörterbuch
zum bequemen Nachschlagen für Anfänger, nach dem Alphabet
eingerichtet. pp. 224. Three plates of apparatus.

Referred to in Blade's "Depositio Cornuti Typographici" (London, 1885).

——— Neues theoretisch-practisches Lehrbuch der Buchdruckerkunst für angehende Schriftsetzer und Drucker in den
Buchdruckereyen, in welchem auch alles, was denselben von
andern Wissenschaften, Kunst- und Gewerbsfächern, die mit der
Buchdruckerkunst in naher Verwandtschaft oder Verbindung
stehen, zu wissen nöthig ist, deutlich erkläret wird. Nebst
beigefugtem ausführlichen Formatbuche. Wien 1810. 8vo.
Vol. i., pp. 220 and 1 plate of Type-specimens. Vol. ii., Titel
und Erklärung, 2 leaves ; text, pp. 108 ; schemes of imposition,
pp. xxxiii.; 1 plate of correction-marks, and an engraved plate
of the mechanism of a press.

Both volumes are chiefly practical.

TAILLANDIER (A.). Procès d'Estienne Dolet, imprimeur à Lyon,
1543-1546. Paris : 1836. 12mo.

This incident has been exhaustively treated by Chancellor R. C. Christie, in his
"Life of E. Dolet," published in 1880.

——— Résumé historique de l'introduction de l'Imprimerie à Paris.
Paris : 1837. 8vo. pp. 58 and facsimile.

The details relating to the commence-
ment and introduction of Printing in
Paris are clearly indicated. In 1460,
Nicholas Jenson, the coin engraver, was,

it is stated, sent from Paris to Mayence
to learn the new invention, but this
journey appears to have been without
result. M. Madden, however, who has

devoted great research to the elucidation of this subject, altogether denies in his "Lettres d'un Bibliographe," 1878, that Jenson was sent on this mission. *See* MADDEN (J. P. A.), *ante.* In 1469, however, the rector of the University, M. Guillaume Fichet, was the means of bringing three Germans to Paris—Ulrich Gering, Martin Grantz, and Michael Friburger, who commenced printing in 1470. The hypothesis that the Brabançon Josse Bade, of Asche, established the first printing-office at Paris is *not* generally believed,—a supposition not, at any rate, very logical, since printing was introduced into Belgium earlier than in Paris.

TAKEL. Typographiæ Encomium. Amstelædami : 1680. 4to.

Four leaves, signed Joannes Takel.

TALBERT. Stationers' Tables : for Stationers, Printers, and all connected with the Paper Trade. London : 1875. 32mo. pp. 11.

Contains fourteen tables, and a list of paper-makers and their mill numbers, &c.

TALLON (Eugène). La Presse en 1631. Paris : 1870. 8vo.

TAMBRONI (Clotilde). Elegia greca in onore del celebre tipografo Giambatista Bodoni con la versione italiana di Gius. Maria Pagnini. Parma : 1795. 4to.

TANGANELLI (Ulisse). Canto del Tipografo Italiano. Firenze : 1879. 8vo, pp. 16.

This is a poem of 54 lines in commemoration of the Typographic Industrial Exhibition inaugurated at Milan on the 3rd of August, 1878. It is dedicated by the author to " Italian printers, who practise their art to their own credit and the glory of their country." It is preceded by an introductory letter to Signor Landi, the editor of the *Arte della Stampa,* and is printed with the type used for the production of that journal. The edition was limited to 150 numbered copies. The poem consists of an impassioned eulogium of the art of printing, which is exalted by the author above the antique glories of Babylon, Egypt, and Greece, and characterised as the only art that can restrain the tooth of Time, and enchain in fetters of lead the fugitive thought as it becomes embodied in words.

"Tu sola, Arte mirabile,
l' edace tempo sai frenar ; tu sola,
Chiusa nei plumbei vincoli
l' idea fuggente che si fa parola."

The varied services that printing has rendered to mankind are enumerated, among which its power to dispel the darkness of priestly bigotry and political tyranny is dwelt upon with emphasis ; and the poem concludes with a festive couplet, of which the following is a rendering :—

" Meanwhile for us the foaming cup
   Of Eastern France our goblet brims,
   And fervently we offer up
   To Art and Honour sacred hymns !"

We scarcely need add that the type and presswork are worthy of the repute of the printer, Sig. Landi.

TANTZ. Schrift- und Druck-Proben aus der neu errichteten Buchdruckerei von A. Tantz & Comp. Weimar : 1835. 8vo.

TARBÉ. Epreuves de Caractères, fleurons, ornements typographiques, etc. E. Tarbé & Cie., successeurs de Firmin Didot, Molé, Crosnier, Everat. Paris : 1839. 8vo.

TARBOURIECH (A.). Les livres d'œuvre au 16me siècle. Paris : 1865. 8vo.

TARIF & Annexe des prix de main d'œuvre typographique adopté par les chambres Syndicales patronales et ouvriers à Rouen. Rouen : 1877. 8vo.

TARIF. Entwurf zu einem allgemeinen Buchdrucker-Tarif (Verband). Leipzig : April, 1876.

TARIFBEWEGUNG und Arbeitseinstellung der Buchdruckergehülfen in Zürich. Zürich : 1875. 8vo. pp. 42. [Reprinted from Böhmer's " Arbeiterverhältnisse."]

TASCHENAGENDA für Buchdrucker.—*See* WALDOW.

TASSIS (S. A.). Guide du Correcteur et du Compositeur, donnant la solution des principales difficultés pour l'emploi des lettres majuscules et minuscules dans l'écriture et l'imprimerie. 6me édition, revue et augmentée. Paris : 1862. 12mo.

The first edition bears the date 1852. The seventh edition was issued with the following title :—

———— Guide du Correcteur, ou Complement des grammaires et des lexiques, donnant la solution des principales difficultés pour l'emploi des lettres majuscules et minuscules dans l'écriture et dans l'imprimerie. 7me édition, revue et augmentée. Paris : 1877. 12mo. pp. 124.

TAUBERT (W.). Gutenberg-Lieder. Op. 51. Berlin : 1840. 4to.

TAUCHNITZ (Karl). Proben aus der Schriftgiesserei von Karl Tauchnitz in Leipzig : 1831. pp. 82. 8vo.

The founder of this firm was the celebrated Karl Christoph Traugott Tauchnitz, born in 1761. He was instructed as a printer in Leipzig and Berlin, and commenced business on his own account in the former city in 1792. In 1798, he added bookselling to his vocations, and in 1800, typefounding. In 1816, he established the first stereotype foundry in Germany. His son, Baron Christian Bernhard, was the projector and publisher of the "Collection of English Authors," the thousandth volume of which series,—the New Testament authorised Version, with various readings, from the most celebrated original texts,—was issued in 1869.

TAURINIUS (C. F.). Der Autor in der Klemme, oder aufgesetzte Zwiebelfische für die .Buchdruckerwelt. Eine Autobiographie. Winterthur : 1841. 8vo.

TAYLOR (C. L. F.). Typographical Pronouncing System of Reading. London : 1853. 8vo.

TEARS of the Press, The ; with Reflections on the present State of England. London : 1681. 4to. pp. 9.

On the enormities of an unlicensed press, said to have been written by J. Whitlock.

TEECKELENBURGH (H. v.). Epreuves des caractères français de l'imprimerie H. v. Teeckelenburgh. La Haye : 1810. 8vo.

———— Proeven van Holland, en vreemde Letteren. La Haye : 1811. 8vo.

[TEISSIER (G. F.)]. Essai philologique sur les commencemens de la

Typographie à Metz, et sur les Imprimeurs de cette Ville. Metz et
Paris : 1828. 8vo. pp. 294, portrait, and facsimiles.

The date of the earliest printed book at Metz is given as 1482. All the printers
from that time to 1828 are placed on record.

TELLE (T.). Enseignement de la typographie et des écritures euro-
péennes. Modifications et corrections proposées dans les écritures
et dans les caractères typographiques en usage. Paris : 1848.
.pp. 18.

TENTZEL (Wilhelm E.). Dissertatio de inventione artis typographicæ
in Germania. Gothæ: 1700. [In Wolf, "Monumenta Typographica," vol. ii., pp. 644–704.]

—— Discours von Erfindung der löblichen Buchdruckerkunst in
Teutschland bei Gelegenheit ihres anscheinenden dritten Jubel-
jahres kurtz und gründlich entworfen. Gotha : 1700. 12mo.
pp. 96.

This work has recently been shown to
have an important bearing upon the
controversy as to the origin of printing.
Lersner published in 1706 his "Chronica
der Stadt Frankfurt a. M." (Frankfurt,
fo.), and in his preface states that he
made use of the many Collectanea of
J. F. Faust von Aschaffenburg. He
devotes a chapter to the members of the
House Limpurg, saying therein that the
noble families of Frankfurt are famous
for their inventions of new sciences;
"and especially Herr Zumjungen zu
Gudenberg invents printing, which Johannes Faust von Aschaffenburg assists
afterwards in cultivating." Treating
subsequently of the question of the invention of printing he quotes Authæus's
"Warhafftige Historia von Erfindung,"
1681, and this is an extract from the
Discours of Tentzel, which ascribes the
invention to Faust. Lersner shows that
Tentzel is entirely wrong. He says: "The
Fausts von Aschaffenburg are a very old,

honest, and distinguished family, who
have always existed on their income or
have died in the employ of great lords
and towns. Where the first lived cannot
be well indicated; I deplore the negli-
gence of my ancestors in this respect, but
it may be through the length of time the
documents have been lost. I have to
regard Johann Faust, who died in 1420,
as the founder of the family ; his son was
joint proprietor in the printing-office in
the town of Mentz. Some would have
and make him against his will an inventor, though he only helped with his
means and good advice in the matter."
Mr. Hessels shows that the remarks of
this author concerning the celebrated lawsuit are eminently untrustworthy; yet
indirectly they form a contribution to the
history of the subject. It is most omin-
ous, he says, that in none of the statements ascribed to the elder Faust von
Aschaffenburg is there any mention of
the instrument of the lawsuit of 1455.

TER BRUGGEN (Edouard). Histoire métallique et Histoire de la
Gravure d'Anvers, appuyées par des pièces et des documents.
Anvers : 1875. 8vo. pp. 308.

Pp. 113–302 contain an account of the works of Flemish engravers who were
members of the Guild of St. Luke.

TERNAUX-COMPANS (H.). Notice sur les Imprimeries qui existent
ou ont existé hors de l'Europe. Paris : [1842]. 8vo. pp. 48.

—— Notice des Imprimeries qui existent ou ont existé en Europe.
Paris : 1843. 8vo. pp. 146 and 2 plates.

Printed originally in the "Nouvelles
Annales des Voyages et des Sciences
géographiques," vols. iii. and iv., Paris,
1842-3. Additions to each of the above

works were published in the *Journal de
l'amateur de Livres*, 1849-50, and were
revised and issued with the following
title :—

—— Notice sur les Imprimeries qui existent ou ont exist en

Europe et hors de l'Europe. (Supplément.) Paris : 1849. 8vo.
pp. 20.
Only 100 copies printed.

—— Nouvelles Additions à la Notice sur les Imprimeries. Paris :
1860. 8vo. pp. 19.
Only 100 copies printed.

TERPAGER (Peter). Ripæ Cimbricæ seu urbis Ripensis in Cimbria
sitæ descriptio ex antiquis monumentis, bullis, diplomatibus eruta
et variis iconibus æri incisis. Flensburgi : 1736. 4to.
Section v. is headed " De Typographia." The first printer in Ripen (Jutland)
was Matthew Brandt, 1504.

—— De typographiæ natalibus in Dania, schedula historica quam
auxiliante Deo et annuente facultate philosophica publico con-
flictui sistit Laurentius Terpager Pet. F. Respondente per-amico
viro juvene Johanne Frisio, Joh. F. in auditorio collegii medicei.
Havniæ : 1707. 4to. pp. 16.

TERZUOLO. Note sur la presse à tiroir, nouvelle presse inventée.
Paris : 1842. 8vo.

TESTE, CAMPBELL, & CO. Nouveau Système de Stéréotypie. Paris :
1829.
A folio broadside referring to the then recently introduced paper process.

TETTAU (W. von). Ueber einige bis jetzt unbekannte Erfurter
Drucke aus dem 15. Jahrhundert. Erfurt : 1870. 8vo. pp. 160.
Only fifty copies printed.

TETTERODE (N.). Catalogue raisonné des Types Égyptiens Hiératiques
de la Fonderie de N. Tetterode à Amsterdam. Dessinés par W.
Pleyte. Leyde : 1865. 4to. pp. viii. 40, and 3 folding plates.

—— De tegenwoordige stand van het Lettergieters bedrijf. Amsterdam : 1861. 8vo.

LEIPZIG : 1495-1521.

THANNER (Jacob).
This printer's device, which is annexed, consists of the emblem of the globe and
cross, with the Gothic letters I t on either side ; the whole in white, on a black
ground.

THAUSING (Moritz). Dürer, Geschichte seines Lebens und seiner Kunst, mit Illustrationen. Leipzig : 1876. 8vo. pp. 536.

This work is considered to be the best that has been written about Dürer. It was out of print for some time, but a second revised edition has been published.

THAYER (William M.). The Printer-Boy ; or, how Benjamin Franklin made his Mark. An example for youth. London : [1861]. 8vo. pp. xvi. 264, frontispiece, and 6 plates.

—— How Benjamin Franklin, the Printer-Boy, made his Mark. An example for youth. London and Edinburgh : 1875. 8vo. 4 leaves and pp. 264.

An interesting little romance, in which the facts of Franklin's early life are claimed to be truthfully narrated.

THEATRUM virorum eruditorum qui speciatim typographiis laudabilem operam præsiderunt. Nurembergi : 1720. 8vo.

THEINHARDT (F.). Liste der hieroglyphischen Typen aus der Schriftgiesserei des Herrn F. Theinhardt in Berlin. Mit Vorwort von Prof. R. Lepsius. Berlin : 1876. 4to.

Six pages of text and 24 of plates, the latter containing specimens of 1,380 separate types or signs. The hieroglyphs of Theinhardt differ from those of other foundries by the fact that they are only given in outlines, not in full black bodies, to make them harmonise better with the appearance of common modern types.

—— Liste der Typen Assyrischer Keilschrift. Berlin : 1877. Large 8vo. pp. 10.

A list of the Assyrian cuneiform characters, produced in the typefoundry of Herr Theinhardt, of Berlin.

THENOT (Jean Pierre). Cours complet de Lithographie, contenant la description des moyens à employer et des accidents à éviter pour dessiner sur pierre, 1re livraison. Paris : 1836. 4to. pp. 8 ; five lithographic examples.

COLOGNE : 1470-1483.

THERHOERNEN (Arnold).

Nothing is known about the birthplace of this printer, but from his name it may be fairly supposed that he was a native of the Netherlands. His printing-office at Cologne was in activity as early as 1470. Some writers think that he was the first printer who introduced the numbering in types of the pages of books, as the very first production from his press — the "Sermo ad populum predicabilis in festo presentationis beatissime virginis Marie"—is numbered, not at the top, but on the centre of the exterior margin. He was the first also to introduce running titles, as may be seen in his "Quæstiones de XII. quodlibet," of Thomas Aquinas, 1471, folio. The first book printed in colours by Therhoernen is "**Liber de** Remediis utriusque fortune," 1471. The connexion between Therhoernen and the Brethren of Common Life is undoubtedly established by a similarity of **types,** which **cannot** be explained unless **by the** admission of a typefounder common to both. Van der Meersch (" Recherches sur la vie et les travaux des Imprimeurs Belges et Néerlandais établis à l'étranger," Gand, 1856, 8vo.) assumes that the Brethren were the pupils of Therhoernen,

but the probability **is** that he was **himself** either a member of their **fraternity** or originally one of their workmen. **The** editions *sine nota* of the Brethren are distinguished by the constant use of the cursive *a,* while in Therhoernen's books it is mixed with the doubly-divided Gothic **a.** The foregoing device consists of a triangle, of which **the** two upright sides **are** prolonged **with a** crosslet ; in the **centre a** star ; **at the sides, the** Gothic **letters t ;** the **whole on a very** small **shield,** hanging from **a broken stump.**

THEUNE **(C. H.).** De Typographiæ in rem Christianam meritis et peccatis, programma. Soraviæ : 1740. 4to.

THIBOUST **(C. L.).** De Typographiæ excellentia, carmen notis **Gallicis** illustratum, Ludovico XV. dicatum à C. L. Thiboust, nova editio à Cl. Carolo Thiboust, regis, necnon Academiæ Parisiensis fusore-typographo, ac bibliopolâ. Cum effigie Autoris. Parisiis : 1754. 8vo. pp. 28 and three plates.

Translated by his son under the title, "L'Exc-llence de l'imprimerie." There is a second title-page in French. Prefixed is an engraved portrait of the **author,** with an epitaph underneath, by **Thiboust** Fils, printers to the King, as follows :—

Docte, enjoué, plaisant, **ce** vieillard agréable,
Fut un mortel, humain, généreux, secourable,
Bon père. tendre ami, sans détour et sans fard,
Et celui de nos jours qui sût le mieux son Art.

Th2 poem gives a technical account of the different processes involved in printing, and is illustrated with engravings. To these are appended quaint mottoes, such as—

The Founder.
Le fondeur donne au caractère
La justesse et la netteté,
Par son art il fait qu'on revère
L'impression pour sa beauté.

The Compositor and Pressman.
L'airain, le marbre, le pinceau,
Présentent à nos yeux un spectacle admirable ;
Mais ce que ces Arts ont de beau
Cède à l'impression plus noble et plus durable.
Cet art ingénieux sçait braver le dessin,
Par son secours l'esprit en devient plus divin,
Il conduit les sçavans au temple de mémoire,
Il fait de l'univers et l'amour et la gloire.

The family **of** THIBOUST occupies a distinguished **place in** the list of French typographers. **It** began with Guillaume Thiboust, **a** printer **of the** 16th century, who wrote, in 1544, **a book** called " Les Complaintes d'une Dame surprise d'Amour." His son, Samuel Thiboust, was the printer to the University, and published the celebrated "Mythologie, ou 'Explication des Fables," by Baudouin, **in** folio, with engravings, and the " Histoire d'Espagne," by Turguet, in two volumes folio. He was succeeded, **as** printer to the University, by his **son** Claude Thiboust, who died suddenly at Passy, in 1667. The posthumous son of the latter, Claude Louis Thiboust, passed as master of arts in 1685, and then became printer and publisher to the University. He turned his attention to typefounding, with much success, in **1694.** The decree appointing him printer to **the** University thus refers to his predecessors : " Qui contra quam cæteri librarii solent, plus in arte suâ nominis ac famæ quam divitiarum sibi suisque comparare studuerint." This printer issued several splendid editions of the classics. He **was** a good Latin and Greek scholar, and wrote in the former language the above-cited poem, and printed it **in** Paris, 1718, 8vo. He died in 1737. His son, Claude Charles Thiboust, was his successor, and in reputation his rival. He was likewise **a** man of good education. He translated **the** Latin poem of his father, and reprinted it with his own translation in 1754. In 1748 Claude C. Thiboust compiled a list of 409 " Libraires et Imprimeurs de Paris, reçus depuis 1689 jusqu'en 1748." He evinced a great veneration for the memory of his father, and had a portrait of him engraved by the celebrated engraver Daullé, placing beneath it four elegiac lines written by himself.

He also printed a "Traduction littérale et poétique des Psaumes de David; suivant la Vulgate" by Pepin, in 1744. Some days after, he himself satirised this translation in a "Lettre à un ami." He rendered into French prose various Latin verses, which he found in the cloisters of the Chartreux de Paris, and wrote the life of St. Bruno. Two editions of this work were issued, one in quarto in 1755 with the Latin original at the beginning, and engravings by Chauvan ; and the other, also in quarto, without engravings. He was engaged on a translation of Horace, when he died, in 1757.

THIELE (J. M.).—*See* RUMOHR and THIELE.

THIERRY-POUX (O.).—*See* CORRARD DE BRÉBAN.

THOMAS (Isaiah). The History of Printing in America, with a Biography of Printers and an Account of Newspapers ; to which is prefixed a concise View of the Discovery and Progress of the Art in other Parts of the World. 2 vols. Worcester [Massachusetts] : 1810. 8vo.

The following extracts from the preface explain the object and scope of this work :—

"Amidst the darkness which surrounds the discovery of many of the arts, it has been ascertained that it is practicable to trace the introduction and progress of Printing, in the northern part of America, to the period of the Revolution. A history of this kind has not, until now, been attempted, although the subject, in one point of view, is more interesting to us than to any other nation.

"I am sensible that a work of this kind might, in other hands, have been rendered more interesting. It has a long time been the wish of many that some person distinguished for literature would bring it forward : but, as no one has appeared who was disposed to render this service to the republic of letters, the partiality of some of my friends led them to entertain the opinion, that my long acquaintance with Printing must have afforded me a knowledge of many interesting facts, and pointed out the way for further inquiry, and that, therefore, I should assume the undertaking. Thus I have been, perhaps too easily, led to engage in a task which has proved more arduous than I had previously apprehended and which has been attended with much expense.

"It is true that, in the course of fifty years, during which I have been intimately connected with the art, I became acquainted with many of its respectable professors, some of whom had, long before me, been engaged in business. From them I received information respecting the transactions and events which occurred in their own time, and also concerning those of which they received the details from their predecessors. By these means I have been enabled to record many circumstances and events which must soon have been buried in oblivion. My long acquaintance with printing, and the researches I made in several of the colonies before the Revolution, certainly afforded me no inconsiderable aid in this undertaking ; and, to this advantage, I may add, and I do it with sincere and grateful acknowledgments, that I have received the most friendly attention to my inquiries from gentlemen in different parts of the United States.

"The history of printing in America, I have brought down to the most important event in the annals of our country—the Revolution. To have continued it beyond this period, all will admit would have been superfluous."

The original work is now rarely met with. Hence its republication, under the following title :—

――― The History of Printing in America, with a Biography of Printers, and an Account of Newspapers. Second edition, with the Author's Corrections and Additions, and a Catalogue of American Publications previous to the Revolution of 1776.

Published under the supervision of a special Committee of the American Antiquarian Society. 2 vols. Albany : 1874. 8vo.

It is stated in the preface that the late Dr. Isaiah Thomas left behind him a corrected copy of his work, with the view of issuing a new and revised edition, and the Committee appointed to supervise this republication have endeavoured to carry out, as nearly as practicable, the intentions of the author, thus disclosed.

It appears that the late Mr. Joel Munsell, who printed this edition, had long held a similar purpose in mind, and had made collections with reference to it ; but since the American Antiquarian Society, of which he was a member, decided to put to press the revised copy left in their possession, he had given the advantage of his information and judgment to that object, having himself joined the Committee in charge of the publication.

THOMPSON.   Recueil de vignettes gravées sur bois et polytypées par Thompson.   Paris : 1828.   4to.—1831, 4to.—1832, 4to.—1833, 8vo.

THOMPSON (Edward Maunde).   Letters of Humphrey Prideaux to John Ellis, 1674-1722, edited by E. M. Thompson.   London : printed for the Camden Society, 1875.   4to.

With a letter, dated Jan. 13, 1679-80, he encloses, "The state of ye affair of Printeing in ye University of Oxford," relating that in 1672 John, Bishop of Oxford, Sir Joseph Williamson, Sir Leoline Jenkins, and Dr. Thomas Yate, took upon themselves the charge of the University Press, and imported type and materials from Germany, France, and Holland, at an expense of over £4,000. Having engaged with some booksellers, and printed Bibles which sold for considerably less than formerly, the King's Printers, who had the monopoly of that book, had summoned them before the Privy Council for infringing their right. Prideaux, with the idea of showing the right of Oxford University to the liberty of printing, mentions the grant of Edward I. giving that University the privilege of "multiplying and encreasing of bookes by writeing," and recites the exploded story of Atkyns, that Corsellis printed at Oxford in 1468.

THON (Tha.).   Lehrbuch der Kupferstecherkunst, der Kunst in Stahl zu stechen und in Holz zu schneiden, frei nach dem Französischen. Weimar : 1831.   8vo., with eight illustrations.

THONNELIER.   Notice sur les Presses Mécaniques de M. Thonnelier, breveté d'invention et d'importation.   Paris : 1832.   8vo.

THORNE (Samuel).   Samuel Thorne, Printer.   London : 1875.   8vo. pp. 191.

Thorne's father was one of the founders of the sect of "Bible Christians," first established October 9, 1815, at Lake Farm, his residence. Samuel Thorne became printer and publisher to the sect, and edited their various magazines and publications. This memoir of him is written by Samuel Thorne, of Bodmin, his son, we presume : it is rather an account of him as a "Bible Christian" than as a printer.

THOROWGOOD (W.)   Specimen of Printing Types.   London : 1827. 8vo.

THOROWGOOD (W.) & Co.   New Specimen of Printing Types, late R. Thorne's, No. 2, Fann-street, Aldersgate-street.   London : 1821.   8vo.

The following note has an historical interest :—"To Printers.—Fann Street, London, Jan. 1, 1821. Gentlemen, I cannot omit the opportunity in presenting my first specimen to your notice, to return my most sincere thanks to the Profession for that portion of their Patronage which Mr. Thorne, &c., &c.—Your very humble I have received since my succession to servant, W. Thorowgood."

—— Additions to the Specimen of the Fann-street Letter Foundry, London. W. Thorowgood, Letter Founder to His Majesty. 1830. 8vo.

It is stated in the Specimen Book that "a New Edition of the Greek, Hebrew, and Foreign Characters of the Polyglot Foundry, late the property of Dr. Fry, is in preparation."

—— Fann-street Letter Foundry, London. Thorowgood's Specimen of Greek, Hebrew, and Foreign Characters, late the property of Dr. Edmund Fry. London: 1830. 8vo. Title and four pages.

The Fann-street letter-foundry, as already stated, was originated by Thomas Cottrell, a pupil of the first Caxton. Afterwards it was purchased by Robert Thorne, after whose death it was bought by W. & F. Thorowgood.—*See* Fry & Steel, and Reed & Sons, *ante*.

THORWALDSEN. Guttenbergs Denkmal. Glogau 1837.

Two folio sheets, one representing the statue of Gutenberg, the other the bas-reliefs on the same. These plates were designed under the direction of Thorwaldsen, by Guglielmi, in Rome, and lithographed by Hanfstaengl, in Dresden. An account of the statue itself will be found *ante*, *sub voce* GUTENBERG, vol. i., p. 289.

THOU (de). Observations sur quelques endroits des Annales typographiques de Maittaire. Paris: [s.d.]. 4to. pp. 40.

THOXHEN (James Arnold). Printing in Paris Fourteen Years Ago.

This constitutes a series of extremely well-written articles in the *Printers' Journal* (in 1868), new series, vol. i., pp. 262, 277, 294, 326, 342, 377, 390; vol. ii., p. 2. There is an abundance of practical information concerning French printing-offices.

THUN (Johann Nicolaus). Neu verbessertes auf der löblichen Kunst der Buchdruckerey nützlich zu gebrauchendes Formatbuch ; dem beygefüget etliche oriental. Alphabeten, Abdruck einiger Schriftproben ; nebst dem gebräuchlichen Deposition-Büchlein in Nieder- und Ober-Sächsischer Sprache. Leipzig and Lübeck : 1724. 8vo.

THUNOT (E.). Association des imprimeurs de Paris. Rapport sur le Traité de la typographie de Henri Fournier. Paris : 1854. 12mo. pp. 8.

—— Compte-Rendu des Travaux de l'Association des Imprimeurs de Paris pendant l'année 1856. Paris : 1857. 8vo. pp. 8.

Contains an account of the proceedings of the Printers' Association of Paris, held on the 20th January, 1857.

—— Tarif révisé des prix de composition, adopté dans la conférence mixte de 1850. Paris : 1850. 8vo. pp. 7.

THURA (Alberti). Idea historiæ litterariæ Danorum. Hamburgi : 1723. 8vo.

Reprinted from the "Bibliopholies et Typographeis Danorum."

THÜRINGISCH-ERFURTER Gedenkbuch.—*See* GEDENKBUCH.

THUVIEN (Th.). Nouvelle presse lithographique d'environ 100 kilogrammes, format demie-tellière. Paris : 1850. 4to.

TIBERINA. Caratteri, fregi, e vignette della tipografia Tiberina. Roma : 1854. 4to.

TICOZZI (Stefano). Dizionario degli architetti, scultori, pittori, intagliatori, etc. d' ogni età e d' ogni nazione. Milano : 1830-33. 8vo. 4 vols.

—— Storia dei letterati e degli artisti del departimento della Piave, di Stefano Ticozzi. Belluno : 1813. 4to.

The author quotes Cambruzzi, and supports his arguments concerning the invention of typography by Castaldi.

TIEDEMANN (D.). Zur Geschichte der Buchdrucker-Privilegien. [In "Hessische Beiträge zur Gelehrsamkeit u. Kunst." 1784: 2 parts, pp. 249.]

TIELE (P. A.). De eerste Boekdrukkers te Amsterdam. [In " Bibliographische Adversaria," 1873, No. 5. s'Gravenhage.]

—— L'Histoire de l'Imprimerie en Hollande. [In *Le Bibliophile belge*, viii⁰ année (1873). pp. 16-23.]

—— Les premiers imprimeurs de l'Université de Leide (les Silvius, Christoph Plantin, les Ravelinghen). [In *Le Bibliophile belge*, fourth year, 1869. pp. 112-119, pp. 141-145, and pp. 157-160.]

TILETAN. Catalogus librorum qui in officina Fs. Lud. Tiletani prodierunt, ibidem nati, vel emendati, vel alioque illustrati et excusi. Parisiis : 1546. 8vo.

TIMBS (John). Wonderful Inventions. London : 1867. Crown 8vo.

Pages 54 to 75 give an account of the history of printing, with ten woodcuts.

TIMPERLEY (Charles H.). A Dictionary of Printers and Printing, with the Progress of Literature, Ancient and Modern, Bibliographical Illustrations, &c., &c. London : 1839. 8vo. pp. vi. 996, with 11 plates.

One of the most interesting works a printer can possess : while laying no claim to originality, it is full of anecdote and historical facts. There are the portraits of four printers, viz., John Nichols, W. Bulmer, Henry Fisher, and James Montgomery. The title is printed in red and black, and bears the motto :—"If asked, why printers and booksellers in particular?—I answer, they are a valuable class of the community—the friendly assistants, at least, if not the patrons of literature—and I myself one of the fraternity. Let the members of other professions, if they approve of the suggestion, in like manner, record the meritorious actions of their brethren."

—— The Printers' Manual : containing Instructions to Learners, with Scales of Imposition, and numerous Calculations, Recipes, and Scales of Prices in the principal towns of Great Britain ;

together with Practical Directions for conducting every department of a Printing-office. London: 1838. 8vo. pp. 116 and frontispiece.

The frontispiece is a wood-engraving of "the Composing-room" showing frames, bulks, cases, forms, galleys, chases, and a compositor at work.

In the introduction it is stated that this compilation is not offered as a new work, nor to give the experienced printer any instructions for the guidance of his business, but with the view of collecting such information as has been accumulated by the labours of those who have written before on the subject. Many tables, however, have been added (it is stated) which "have not as yet appeared in a Printers' Grammar, new tables of calculations, plans of imposition, and scales of prices."

The following criticism, by Timperley, of previous writers on the same subject may be worth reproduction:—"The first work written in England expressly for the use of the trade, was 'Smith's Printers' Grammar,' 1755, which consequently laid the foundation for all his successors; Luckombe's 'History and Art of Printing,' 1770; Stower's 'Printers' Grammar,' 1808; Johnson's 'Typographia; or, the Printers' Instructor,' 1824; and Hansard's 'Typographia,' 1825. Stower says that Smith's was the foundation of his work; Luckombe compiled his work from three sources, namely Ames's 'Typographical Antiquities' for the historical part, Smith's 'Printers' Grammar' for the practical part of the composing department, and Moxon's 'Mechanick Exercises' for the presswork. It is very clear that Luckombe made free use of his predecessor as far as he went; for, upon a close comparison, much of Luckombe will be found to be plagiarised from Smith, altered a little in arrangement and phraseology; and that, in his turn, Stower copied from Luckombe. Smith, from his own acknowledgment, appears to have compiled his book under very adverse circumstances, and solely with a view to relieve himself from his embarrassments. It is plain he only went half through with his design, since his volume treats only upon the business of a compositor, not mentioning once press or pressman. Hansard says that his work is partly founded upon the basis of the 'Printers' Grammar' published by Mr. Stower; and Johnson acknowledges the sources whence he compiled his 'Typographia.' Thus it plainly appears, that each writer of a Printers' Grammar has not hesitated to take from his predecessor all that he thought requisite to form his own." Timperley begins with an essay on punctuation, and proceeds to composing, imposing, correcting in metal, typographical marks, the reader's vocation, and scales of prices, describing by the way all the chief implements of the art. He then gives directions to pressmen, with a description and views of the Stanhope (omitting the old wooden press on the ground that "at the present day [1838] its use is nearly exploded"), the Columbian, the Albion, and the Imperial presses, with short notes concerning other presses. He treats of presswork in a thoroughly practical manner, and gives various recipes for ink and roller-making, &c. In the "conclusion," he refers to the great progress made during the thirty years previously in fine printing, stating that Baskerville many years before had given the first impulse to improvement, while the exertions of Bensley, Bulmer, and McCreery contributed to give a new tone and character to the profession. The work ends with a list of the technical terms used by printers, which is, by the way, very incomplete.

The "Printers' Manual" is usually bound up with the "Encyclopædia of Literary and Typographical Anecdote" under the circumstances mentioned in the succeeding article; but it does not form an integral part of that work, and the paging, style of composition, &c., are altogether distinct.

——— Encyclopædia of Literary and Typographical Anecdote; being a chronological digest of the most interesting facts illustrative of the history of Literature and Printing, from the earliest period to the present time. Interspersed with biographical sketches of eminent booksellers, printers, type-founders, engravers, bookbinders, and paper-makers of all ages and countries, but especially of Great Britain; with bibliographical and descriptive accounts of their principal productions and occasional extracts from them, including **curious** particulars of the first introduction of printing into various countries, and of **the** books then printed ; notices of early Bibles and liturgies of **all** countries, especially those printed in England or in English ; a history of all the newspapers. periodicals, and almanacks published in this country ; an account **of** the origin and progress of language, writing, and writing materials, the invention of paper, use of paper-marks, &c. Compiled and condensed from Nichols's Literary Anecdotes, and numerous other authorities. Second edition ; to which are added a continuation to the present time, comprising recent biographies, chiefly of booksellers, and a Practical Manual of Printing. London : 1842. Super-royal 8vo. pp. vi. and 996, printed **at** Manchester, with 12 pages added (1 to 12) printed in London.

This is, in reality, the "Dictionary of Printers and Printing," with another title, the quire-stock, or "remainder" having been bought by Mr. H. G. Bohn, who gave the book a new title-page, as above, and added the twelve pages of matter at the end, which contain some meagre particulars of printers and booksellers, from 1839 to 1842. The book was issued with the "Printers' Manual" (see *supra*), interpolated bodily between pages 32 and 33 ; in the re-bound copy at the British Museum, however, the Manual is placed at the end.

The original preface (retained in Bohn's reissue) is dated Manchester, June 1, 1839. It is therein stated that the portion of the work which forms the introduction was delivered as one of **two** lectures in 1828, and the author was induced to pursue the subject further, as a means both of self-instruction and amusement for his leisure hours. "From that time to the present," says Timperley, "scarcely any other object has engrossed more of my attention than that of obtaining every information relative to Printers and Printing. Not aware of the labours that others had performed, and without an assistant, I had many obstacles to contend with, and soon became well convinced that the design I had formed was above the bibliographical acquirements of **a** journeyman printer. Stimulated, however, to proceed, I continued my researches with increased ardour, and, though conscious of not having made the work what it might have been under more favourable circumstances, yet I trust some merit may be thought due for the attempt ; and shall feel gratified, if placed in the field of literature, only as a pioneer, to induce some abler hand to improve the work, and make it more worthy of the literary world and the profession of which it treats.'

The author gives, in the preface, the following account of his early days :—" I received the rudiments of my education at a day-school in my native town, Manchester, and was afterwards removed **to** the free grammar-school under the **Rev.** Thomas Gaskell. Early attached **to** a love of reading, I have remained all my life an ardent inquirer after knowledge. From the month of March, 1810 (being then little more than fifteen years of age), to November 28, 1815, my days were passed in the 33rd Regiment of Foot, from which I obtained my discharge in consequence of wounds received at the battle of Waterloo. During those years I had few facilities of self-improvement. Having been apprenticed to an engraver and copperplate printer, I resumed the latter on returning from the army ; but, from a distaste and other causes which need not be here stated, in the year 1821 I adopted the profession of a letterpress-printer, under indenture, with Messrs. Dicey & Smithson, proprietors of the *Northampton Mercury*, and feel gratified that an opportunity has occurred of publicly recording my gratitude to Mr. Robert Smithson, printer and editor of the *Mercury*, for his uniform kindness during my abode at Northampton, and to whose advice I am solely indebted for a very material change, both in my circumstance and conduct. Adopting the profession of a printer, with the view of affording me that literary information which I so ardently desired, I endeavoured to become acquainted with its history. From this desire arose the "Lectures" at Warwick, the "Songs of the Press" at Nottingham, and finally the "Dictionary of Printers and Printing," with the "Printers' Manual" at Manchester.

The preface occupies 6 pages ; and the introduction "On the Origin of Language and the Modes and Materials used by the Ancients for Transmitting Knowledge before the Invention of Printing," 32 pages. The text begins with a disquisition on the "State of Literature, from the Earliest Period to the Invention of Printing," which occupies pages 33 to 100. The "History of Printing, and Progress of Literature" follows, the first section being devoted to the period from the invention of the art to the abolition of the Star Chamber, in the year 1694. In regard to the controversy respecting the first discoverer, Timperley says:—"The dispute has turned rather on words than facts, and it seems to have arisen from the different definitions of the word 'printing.' If we estimate the discovery from the invention of the principle, the honour is unquestionably due to Laurence Koster, a native of Haarlem, who first found out the method of impressing characters on paper by means of carved blocks of wood. If movable types be considered as a criterion, the merit of the discovery is due to John Gutenberg, of Mentz, and Schœffer, in conjunction with Faust, was the first who founded types of metal." The succeeding sections are headed,

respectively, Fifteenth, Sixteenth, Seventeenth, Eighteenth, and Nineteenth century, but the annals are brought down only to 1838. At the end is "A literary Chronology, showing the progress of English literature from the earliest times to the present; a list of newspapers and periodicals in the course of publication in 1838; a chronological index of the towns and countries in which the art of printing is known to have been exercised, with about 30 pages of general and classified indexes." The book is illustrated with steel and wood engravings, consisting of portraits, &c. Mr. Bohn's fragmentary additions bring the work from 1839 to 1842.

It is interesting to record that Timperley says, in his Introduction, that it was his intention "to give a complete list of the works which had been produced upon the history of printing, with short biographical notices of their authors. This, I found, would have extended the work more than was contemplated; and, indeed, after much labour, I found that I could not, for the present, give them as complete as would have been desired."

———— Songs of the Press, and other Poems relative to the Art of Printers and Printing; also of Authors, Books, Booksellers, Bookbinders, Editors, Critics, Newspapers, &c. Original and selected, with Notes, biographical and literary. London: 1845. 8vo. pp. viii. 208.

This still keeps its place as the best collection of printers' songs written in the English language, but there are French and German works of a similar character that much surpass it in scope and style.

An interesting sketch of Charles H. Timperley, written by Dr. Spencer Hall, appeared in the *Lithographer*, vol. iv., p. 221 (April, 1874), and Mr. W. Blades contributed to the *Printers' Register*, December, 1873, a short memoir, from which the following facts are derived:—

CHARLES H. TIMPERLEY was born in Manchester in 1794. In 1810 he enlisted in the 33rd Regiment of Foot. He fought at Waterloo, and, being wounded, received his discharge in November, 1815. He then became a letterpress printer, serving his time, under indentures, with the proprietors of the *Northampton Mercury*. In 1828, he delivered two lectures upon the Art of Printing, before the Warwick and Leamington Literary Institution, which met with a very favourable reception; and from that time, to

quote his own words, "scarcely any other object engrossed more of my attention than that of obtaining information upon all points concerning printers and printing."

The following is a kindly tribute to the memory of Timperley, from the same article:—"It is more than forty years since a stranger, lame from being long before wounded in battle, limped in the gloom of a winter evening into Nottingham. A load of coals had been put down near the door of Mr. Henson, at the top of the Poultry. Our wayfarer asked if he might be employed in 'getting in' the said coals; and, cheered by an affirmative answer, did the work well, for which he was as cheerfully paid a shilling, that enabled him to secure a simple refection and a bed.

"A few days afterwards he was working by my side in the *Nottingham Mercury* office, on South Parade, and telling me the story of his fortunes. His name was Charles H. Timperley.

"Charles Timperley was neither tall,

stout, nor handsome; but there was something about him that could not but win for him respect and confidence; he had editorial aspirations, and only a few months had passed ere he was foreman in the office of Mr. Kirk, St. Peter's Gate, and editor of a little monthly magazine called the *Nottingham* (or *Nottinghamshire*) *Wreath*. While thus engaged, he married a respectable widow, and shortly afterwards left the town. It **was** little **we** heard of him thence for many years, except that he had been engaged in compiling ' Songs of the Press,' in reality a collection of all the scraps of verse he could gather on the subject ; a thick and masterly volume on the History of Printing, and other works of the same kind, all evincing the most marvellous research and industry, when one day, in the year 1845, as I was sitting **in** my room in London, Mr. Timperley, preceded by his card, came in, and I felt very glad to see him, having often wondered what, after leaving Nottingham, had been his fate.

" His dress, his **address, and tone** altogether, bespoke **the** gentleman **and** scholar. My memory of his having **in** his adversity earned that honest shilling at the top of the Poultry, by getting in the coals, added greatly in my eyes to his manly dignity ; and I felt not a little complimented when he told me that the object of his visit was not only to con- gratulate me on my own progress in life, but to ask if I would give him liberty to quote some verse of mine in a book he was then editing, on the Scenery of the English Lakes.

" ' And what, sir,' I cordially asked, ' may be your position **in life, after all your** trials and struggles **partially known to** us?'

" There was a modest tone of satisfac- tion and cheerfulness in his reply, that he was enjoying a regular engagement under a large publishing firm as general editor, at **a** handsome salary, and that his life altogether was as comfortable as he could wish it to be **at** his age, and in his circumstances.

" **On** inquiring for him in after-years, I was told Mr. Timperley was dead ; but he will never die to me. I see him often in all his vicissitudes—the printer's boy, the wounded soldier, the limping compositor on tramp ; the foreman and humble con- ductor in Nottingham of the *Wreath ;* the industrious and successful *collabo- rateur* and chronicler in London ; the genuine example throughout of an intel- ligent and most worthy man ; but in **no** phase does he to my mind ever seem more respectable than in the practical rebuke he made of himself to all fastidious and idle vagabonds, when on that cold and dreary evening, in the Poultry, he got in Mr. Henson's coals rather than beg."

In publishing the preceding, the *Litho- grapher* gave some extracts from Curwen's " History of Booksellers " (Chatto & Windus), which furnish the information that has often been sought as to the original cause of the troubles and the ultimate position of Charles Timperley. It appears that the printers of the " Dictionary of Printers and Printing " (Bankes & Co.) also carried on an immense trade upon a thoroughly repre- hensible system. The managing partner of the firm was one Hayward, and, to quote the work named, " he opened shops in various places, placed his own servants in possession, and made them accept bills to a very large amount. These bills were discounted at the Manchester Bank, and, when the crash came, the bank was a creditor upon the estate to the amount of £120,000, while the London publishers were indebted to the extent of £100,000. Among the shopmen in charge under Hayward's system was Timperley, a printer, and a man of considerable literary ability. To pay the debts contracted through his wholesale acceptance of bills, he consigned his stock to an auctioneer, who, after disposing of it by auction, ran off with the proceeds of the sale. Tim- perley, heart - broken by misfortune, accepted a literary engagement with Fisher & Jackson, of London, and in their service he died."

TIPOGRAFIA del secolo xv.   Milano : 1834.   8vo.

TIPO Italiano non Elzeviriano.   Roma : 1879.   16mo.   pp. 89.
The author is Sr. Centenari, Director of the Elzevir Press at Rome.

TIRABOSCHI (Girolamo).   Catalogo dei libri stampati in Modena, in Reggio, e in altri luoghi di questi ducati nel secolo xv.   [In " Biblioteca Modenese," vol. iv., pp. 368, *et seq.*, and vol. vi., pp. 174.   Modena : 1781.   4to.]

——— Dell' invenzióne della stampa dissertazione. [In " Prodromo della nuova Encylopedia." Siena : 1799. 4to.]

An analysis of the work of Meerman, and a denial of the pretensions, founded upon his "facts," of Haarlem as the birthplace of printing.

——— Notizia istoriche sopra la stamperia di Tripoli, le quali possano servire all' illustrazione della storia tipografica Florentina. Firenzi : 1781. 4to.

——— Storia della letteratura Italiana. 15 vols. Firenze et Milano : 1807–1809. 8vo. pp. 158.

Vol. vi., p. 158, History of Printing in Italy ; pp. 443-450, Chronological list of Italian cities in which Printing was introduced in the fifteenth century, with note of the first book printed in each. Vol. viii., Milano, 1809, 8vo., pp. 201-221, History of Printing in Italy, continued, 1500-1600.

"His diligence, his sagacity, his candour, his constant and patriotic exertions to do justice to the reputation of his countrymen, and to rescue departed worth from ill-merited oblivion, assign to him an exalted situation. The best edition of his Letteratura Italiana is that of Modena, 1787-94, 4to., in 15 volumes, as it contains his last corrections and additions and has the advantage of a complete index. An excellent account of the life and labours of its wonderful author appeared in the fifth volume of the *Athenæum*."— Dibdin (" Bibliomania ").

TISCHBEIN (Johann Heinrich). Die Radier- und Aetzkunst in ihrem ganzen Umfange, oder gründliche Anweisung, alle Arten Zeichnungen mit leichter Mühe auf Kupfer-, Zink- und Zinnplatten sehr täuschend nachzuahmen. Second edition. Zwickau : 1827. 4to. 20 etchings. [First edition, Cassel, 1808.]

LONDON : 1550-1563.

TISDALE (John).

This printer's name is also spelt Tysdall and Tysdale. He was an original member of the Stationers' Company. His house was in Knight Rider Street, and his shop in Lombard Street, in Allhallows Churchyard, near Gracechurch Street.

VOL. III. D

The device consists of the emblem,
"Abraham's Sacrifice." It includes the
figure of the patriarch in the centre,
whose uplifted sword is being arrested

by an angel descending from the skies.
The son of Abraham kneels before an
altar on the left ; on the right is the goat
caught in a thicket.

TISSANDIER (Gaston).   L'Héliogravure, son histoire et ses procédés,
ses applications à l'Imprimerie et à la Librairie. Paris : 1874.
4to. pp. 12.

A paper read at the Conference held at the Cercle de la Librairie, in Paris, on the
24th April, 1874.

——— Histoire de la gravure typographique, Paris : 1875. 4to. pp. 14.

A paper read at the Conference held at the Cercle de la Librairie, in Paris, on the
29th January, 1875.

——— Une Conférence sur l'Héliogravure et ses applications à la
Librairie. Paris : 1874. 12mo. pp. 12.

A report of the discussion on one of the preceding papers.

TISSIER (Louis).   Historique de la gravure typographique sur pierre
et de la Tissierographie. Paris : 1843. 8vo.   pp. 24, and engravings.

TITEL-REGELN, aufgestellt von der Typographischen Gesellschaft in
Leipzig. Leipzig : s. d. [1881]. 4to. 1 leaf.

TOBITT (John H.).   Combination Type : their History, Advantages,
and Application. New York : 1852. 8vo.

An account of an abortive logotype scheme.

TODE (J. C.).   Unpartiiske Tanker om Typographien i Danmark, i
Anledning af et Brevfa en Ubenovnt og et Swar af Hr. Boghandler
Jversen, som findes indrykket i Fyens Stifts Journal Nr. 59 for
1782, fremsatte ved Johan Clemens Tode. Kjobenhavn : 1782.
8vo. pp. 48.

Accounts of Printers in Denmark at the end of the eighteenth century.

TODERINI (A. G.).   Istoria dell' arte impressoria Turchese. [In his
"Letteratura Turchese," part iii. ; also in the French translation
of the same by the Abbé de Cournand, Paris, 1789, vol. iii.]

——— Die Buchdruckerei der Türken.   [In dessen "Literatur der
Türken."   Aus dem Italienischen von P. W. G. Hausleitner.
Bd. ii. part 2.] Königsberg : 1790. Large 8vo.

TOEPFL (F.).   De Latinorum Bibliorum cum nota anni 1462, impresssa
duplici editione Moguntina exercitatio bibliographico - critica.
Ingoldstadt : 1787. 4to.

TOEPPEN (Dr. Max).   Kurze Nachrichten über die Königl. Westpreuss.
Hofbuchdruckerei zu Marienwerder.   Zu deren Säcularfeier zusammengestellt. Marienwerder : 1872. 8vo. pp. 15.

TOIFEL (Wilh. F.). Handbuch der Chemigraphie, Hochätzung in Zink für Buchdruck mittelst Umdruck von Autographien und Photogrammen und direkter Copirung oder Radirung des Bildes auf die Platte (Photochemigraphie und Calcochemigraphie) Wien: 1882. 8vo. 17 sheets, with 14 illustrations.

TOLAND (John). Conjectura verosimilis de prima inventione typographiæ, 1726. [In Wolf, "Monumenta Typographica"; also in Maittaire, "Annales Typographiæ," tome ii.; and in the "Collection of several pieces of John Toland," London, 1726, 8vo.]

TOLLENS (H. C.). Feestzang bij het Vierde Eeuwgetijde van de Uitvinding der Boekdrukkunst. [In "Werken der Hollandische Maatschapij," vol. vii., part i.] Leyden: 1824. 8vo. pp. 20.

TOLMER (A.). Notice sur la machine à composer et à distribuer de M. E. W. Brackelsberg. Rapport à la Chambre des Imprimeurs à Paris. [Reprinted from the *Gutenberg Journal*, No. 52, 1882, and No. 1, 1883.]

TONELLI (Francesco). Cenni storici sull' origine della stampa e sull' artefice che primo fece uso dei caratteri sciolti e fusi. Firenze: 1800. 8vo.

TONELLI (Tommaso). Sunto storico sull' origine della Stampa. [In *Antologia: Giornale di Scienze, Lettere e Arti*, vol. xli., Jan., Feb., and March, 1831. Florence.]
   The author is in favour of Koster's claim, and, from the commencement of his dissertation, entitles him "inventore della stampa."

TONINI (Luigi). Sulle officine Tipografiche Riminesi, Memorie e Documenti. [Extract from the *Atti della Deputazione di Storia Patria per le Provincie di Romagna*.] Bologna: 1866. Large 4to.

TORNABENE (F.). Storia critica della tipografia Siciliana dal 1471 al 1536. Catania: 1839. 8vo.

TÖRNER (Fab.).—*See* ALNANDER.

TORRENTINO (Lorenzo). Annali della Tipografia Fiorentina di Lorenzo Torrentino, Impressore Ducale. Second edition. Florence: 1811. 8vo. pp. lxxxvi. 247.
   Historical and bibliographical.

——— Memoria sulla tipographia Mouregalese dans les Veglie dei pastori della Dora. Turin: 1801. 8vo.

——— *See* MORENI (D.).

TORTEROLI (Tommaso). Sopra la tipografia Savonese. [In "Scritti litterari." Savona: 1860. 16mo.]

TORY (Geoffroy de Bourges). Champ-Flevry, auquel est contenu l'art et science de la vraie proportion des lettres Attiques, ou Antiques, autrement dites Romaines, selon le corps et visage humain. Paris : 1529. Small folio. pp. 8 and lxxx.——Another edition, 1549. 8vo.

This remarkably original work is divided into three parts. The first contains a disquisition upon the proper use of language. The second treats of the origin of capital letters, and institutes a curious and fantastic comparison between them and the true proportions of the human face and frame, with a series of ingenious woodcuts to illustrate the theory. The third part contains accurate drawings of the letters, produced upon a species of chart or diagram in the form of a square, divided into ten lines, perpendicular and transverse, making one hundred square compartments, upon which circles drawn by the compass serve to produce the exact shape of the letters. This division of the book also treats of the pronunciation of peoples of different districts and nations and presents a large number of alphabets of various kinds as well as fanciful letters in arabesque, etc.

The result of this work was an immediate and complete revolution in French typography and orthography—the abandonment of the Gothic and the adoption of a new cut of antique face. Robert Stephens forsook the shapes favoured by his father, and Simon de Colines introduced essential alterations, and the faces of type thus produced were used until near the close of the eighteenth century. The Champ-Fleury also attracted general attention to the proper use in French of the accents, apostrophe, and marks of punctuation, resulting in a remarkable and immediate improvement in the general appearance of the national typography. The publication of this work won for its author the title of King's Printer from the scholarly Francis I., who, despite his especial devotion to the Greek language, recognised the value of such labours in the perfection of the vernacular as an additional mark of

distinction. Tory was elected one of the sworn booksellers of the University of Paris, and, although the regular number—twenty-four—was already full, an additional or extra membership was provided in his honour, to be held by him during his life, and to expire at his death.

The richly-illustrated "Books of Hours" published by Tory are distinguished by a combination of antique art with French grace, and an abandonment of the prevalent Gothic method of ornamentation. A publication in 1533 introduced his own improved system of orthography, the improvement in the use of capitals being especially marked. Tory died about this time and his widow completed and published in 1535 a remarkably fine edition of Diodorus Siculus, which he had commenced.

GEOFFROY TORY, or TORINUS, was born in 1480 of poor parents, in the province of Berry, France, but fortunately obtained patronage which enabled him to attend good schools. He afterwards travelled in Italy, where he had admirable opportunity for pursuing his studies. He began his literary career in Paris in 1505. Having a special fondness for art, he began to practise wood-engraving, and finally determined to pursue art studies in Italy. Here he became much interested in printing. As a wood-engraver he was soon recognised as one of the chief artists of his time. He is supposed to have engraved the elegant antique script used by Henry Stephens. Believing that the undue pre-eminence given by scholars to the Greek and Latin languages was producing a disastrous effect upon the vernacular of his own country, he composed the Champ-Fleury, cited above. He died in 1510.

TOSI (Paolo Antonio). Facsimile di alcune imprese di stampatori Italiani dei secoli xv. e xvi. Milano : 1838. 8vo. pp. 4 and 25 plates.

—— Notizia di una edizione sconosciuta del poema romanzesco " La Spagna"; colla descrizione di un opusculo impresso da Aldo Manuzio nel 1499. Milano : 1835. 8vo.

TOSTO (Stef.). Notizia su l'esistenza d'una tipografia in Catania anteriore di anni 60 al sinodo di M. Torres. Catania : 1839. 8vo.

TOSZKA (gen-Tossek, J. A.). Leitfaden der russischen Sprache für Schriftsetzer, Lithographen, Notenstecher, etc. Leipzig : 1862. 8vo. pp. 60.

Characteristics of European languages (Vol. I.—The Russian language).

TOSZKA (J. A.). Ueber den Satz des Polnischen, mit besonderer Berücksichtigung der Theilung der Worte. Für Correctoren und Schriftsetzer. Leipzig : 1868. 8vo. pp. 14.

An elementary guide for the composition of Polish.

———— Ueber den Satz des Russischen, mit besonderer Berücksichtigung der Theilung der Worte. Für Schriftsetzer und Correctoren. Leipzig : 1868. 8vo. pp. 14.

Elementary rules for the composition of Russian.

TOUR (A) on the Continent. [An article in the *Gentleman's Magazine*, Nov., 1833, p. 406.]

Contains an account of the monuments set up in Haarlem to Koster, a facsimile of his alleged signature, &c.

TRAHAN (P. N.). Statuts et règlements de la communauté des maistres-imprimeurs en taille-douce de la ville et université de Paris. 1754. 8vo.

TRAMAUX-MALHET (J.). Vade-mecum, ou l'indispensable aux typographes (maîtres et ouvriers), libraires, auteurs et journalistes, et en général à toutes les personnes qui impriment ou font imprimer. Louviers : 1843. 18mo. 2 leaves, pp. 386 and 1 tableau.

———— Notice historique sur la typographie, la lithographie, et la gravure sur bois. Louviers. 18mo.

This is an extract from the "Vade-mecum," and is illustrated with engravings on wood, ornamental letters, &c.

TRATTNER (J. T. Edler von). Abdruck der Deutschen Schriften in der Hof-Schriftgiesserey. Wien : 1769. 4to.

———— Feyerliche Rede beim frohen Jubelfeste der 50 Jahre, welche Joh. Thom. Edler von Trattner den 12. März 1798 als Druckerherr und Prinzipal fungirte. Wien : 1798. 8vo.

———— Specimen Characterum Latinorum existentium in Caesarea ac Regio-Aulica typorum Fusura. Vindob.: 1760. 4to.

———— Specimen Characterum Russicorum, Turcicorum, Græcorum, et Hebraicorum in Typorum Fusura. Vindobonæ : 1769. 4to.

TRAUTMANN (F. Chr.). De typographia ab scholis ornamenta copiente, iisdemque gratiam referente disserit ad colloquium familiare d. 25 Apr. 1740, instituendam invitat. Lauban : 1741. pp. 20.

TRENEL (Prosper). Notice sur les produits typographiques de l'imprimerie de Prosper Trenel, admis à l'Expos. Univer. de 1855. St. Nikolas : 1855. 8vo.

TRENTIÈME Année (la) d'Imprimerie. **Couplets** chantés au banquet du 22 Septembre 1850, à la Laitière. Bourg.: 1850. 4½ sheets.

TREUNERT (W.). **Gedichte und Lieder** für Typographen und Schriftgiesser zur vierten Säcularfeier der Buchdruckerkunst. Braunschweig: 1840. 16mo. pp. 56.

TREVES BROS. Le grandi Invenzioni, antiche e moderne. Milan: 1873.

Contains, under the heading of "Typografia," an account of the History of Printing, brought down to a recent date.

TRINCKHUS (G.). Dissertatio de ineptis librorum Titulis. Gerae: [s.d.] 4to.

TRIQUETI (H. de). Gutenberg (Jean Gensfleisch de Sulgeloch) Découverte de l'imprimerie — Discours adressé aux apprentis dans la Séance du Comité de Patronage du 3 Août, 1856. Paris: 1856. 8vo. 8⅞ sheets.

TRITHEMIUS (Joh.). Annales Hirsaugienses. St. Gall: 1690. 4to. 2 vols.

Treats of the block books principally, but refers to the origin of typography. (*See infra.*)

——— Chronicon Sponheimense.

Under date, 1450. Attributes origin of Printing to Gutenberg, at Mentz.

——— Chronicon Hirsaugiense.

Attributes Faust and Schoeffer, 1452.

——— S. Jacobi Wirciburgencis. Compend. Annal. Hist. Origine Regum et Gentis Francorum. Mogunt. Jo. Schöffer, 1515. Folio.

We have not been able to examine these works, which are not in the British Museum. The titles given above are taken from books containing quotations. In regard to the latter, it may be stated that it has lately been shown that there are many inaccuracies in the statements of Trithemius as reproduced by subsequent authors, concerning the origin of printing. Trithemius was one of the most eminent men of the 16th century. He says that the admirable and till then [1450] unheard-of art of printing books by the aid of type was planned and invented by John Gutenberg, who was enabled by the counsel and by the money of John Fust to finish the work they had begun. "They first printed, with engravings of letters on blocks of wood, arranged in proper order in the manner of ordinary manuscripts, the vocabulary then called the 'Catholicon'; but with the letters on these blocks they were not able to print anything else, for the letters were not movable but fixed and unalterable upon the blocks," etc. This would be mere foolish squandering of money in vain efforts to invent xylography, a method of printing then in common use in many cities of Germany, Italy, and Holland. Later on it is said that Schoeffer was the son-in-law of "the first inventor, John Fust," which contradicts the statement above. The general purport of the pretended history is to the effect that Gutenberg, Fust, and Schoeffer may be regarded as co-inventors, but that Schoeffer did the most effective service, by devising "a more easy method of founding types by which he gave the art its present perfection." He must have been misinformed as to the initiatory steps of the process; for it is beyond dispute that cut types were never used. The statements of Trithemius may, however, yet have some value in connexion with some theory not yet definitely propounded.

TROJAN (Karl) und Karl Höger. Almanach für Buchdrucker. 1881.
1. Jahrgang. Vienna: 1881. 16mo. With portrait of Franklin.
pp. xxviii and 120.
Agenda, containing a short biography of Benjamin Franklin, typographical
essays, imposition schemes, etc.

TROSS (Edw.). Ueber die früheste Anwendung der Signaturen in der
Buchdruckerkunst. [In *Serapeum*, vii., pp. 60-61.] Leipzig:
1846.

TROW (John F.). Specimens of Type in the Printing and Stereotyping
Establishment of John F. Trow. New York: 1851. 8vo.

TROYES. Illustration de l'ancienne Imprimerie Troyenne. 210
Gravures sur Bois des xvᵉ, xviᵉ, xviiᵉ, et xviiiᵉ siècles. Publiées
par V. L. Troyes: 1850. 4to. pp. 40, with three preliminary
leaves.

Only eighty copies printed. A very
curious collection of the woodcuts employed by the early printers of Troyes,
Lecoq, Oudot, and Garnier, in the
illustration of their books. They are
engraved by Woériot, Rochienne, Vernier,
etc., and among them is the set of the

well-known "Dance of Death," "Danse
Macabre," taken from sculptures in the
ancient cemetery of the Innocents at
Paris.—*See also* VARUSOLTIS (Varlot
père), "Xylographie de l'imprimerie
Troyenne," 1859, 72 plates; and CORRARD
DE BREBAN.

TRÜBNER'S Bibliographical Guide to American Literature. A classed
List of Books published in the United States of America during
the last forty years. With Bibliographical Introduction, Notes,
and Alphabetical Index. Compiled and edited by Nicholas
Trübner. London: 1859. 8vo.

In the "Contributions towards a
History of American Literature," by
Mr. Benjamin Moran, which forms part
of the Introduction, a chapter is introduced on Printing Presses, and another
on Typography, Typefoundries, &c.

NICHOLAS TRÜBNER was the founder
and chief of the extensive publishing house
of Nicholas Trübner & Co., Ludgate-
hill. He died in 1884, aged 66. He

was a native of Heidelberg, and came
to England in 1847, obtaining employment at Messrs. Longmans. He then
established himself in business on his
own account in Paternoster-row, and
subsequently removed to Ludgate-hill.
From this house was issued *Trübner's
Monthly Record of Oriental Literature*,
a periodical containing much typographical as well as literary, especially
philological, information.

TRUMBULL (George). Pocket Typographia: a brief practical Guide
to the Art of Printing. Albany: 1846. 16mo. pp. 96.
Practical instruction for Compositors. Coarse woodcut frontispiece.

TRUTEBUL (Ludwig), Gründer der ersten Buchdruckerei zu Halberstadt. Portrait lithogr. par C. Ruprecht. (Anno Domini 1520.)
Halberstadt: 1875. 4to.

TSCHASCHLAU (Waldemar de). Essai satirique sur les vignettes,
fleurons, culs-de-lampe, et autres ornements des Livres. Traduction
libre de l'Allemand. Paris: 1873. 8vo. 1 engraving.
Only 200 copies printed.

TSCHERNING'S (Andreas). Lob der Buchdruckerey. Gedruckt zu Bresslau, durch Georgium Baumann, 1640. 4to. 8 leaves.

TUDOT (E.). Description de tous les moyens de dessiner sur pierre, avec l'étude des causes qui peuvent empêcher la réussite de l'impression des dessins. Paris : 1833. 18mo. 6½ sheets.

TUDOT (F.). Traité de Lithographie. Second edition. Paris : 1834. 18mo. 9½ sheets.

TUDOT (J.). Die Lithographie oder Beschreibung aller Mittel auf Stein zu zeichnen. Nach der 2ten verb. und verm. Ausgabe. Stuttgart : 1834. 8vo. 11½ sheets.

TUEFFERD (P. E.). L'Imprimerie à Montbéliard avant la révolution française. Les Imprimeurs, les ouvrages sorties de leurs presses :—Jacques Foillet, Samuel Foillet, Samuel Speckart, Daniel Dietzel, Claude Hyp, Jean Martin Biber, Jean Jacques Biber, Jean Louis Becker. [*Revue d'Alsace*, 1880. pp. 311-336.]

TUER (Andrew White). Bartolozzi and his Works. A biographical and descriptive account of the life and career of Francesco Bartolozzi, R.A. (illustrated) ; with some observations on the present demand for, and value of, his prints ; the way to detect modern impressions from worn-out plates, and to recognise falsely-tinted impressions ; deceptions attempted with prints ; print collecting, judging, handling, &c. ; together with a list of upwards of 2,000—the most extensive record yet compiled—of the great engraver's works. 2 vols. Vol. i., 5 introductory leaves, pp. 211 ; index (sans pagination), pp. 6. Vol. ii., 3 preliminary leaves, pp. 152 ; index, pp. 5. Plates, printed from originals. London : 1881. 4to.

———— Second Edition, revised and corrected, with additional matter. London 1885. 8vo. pp. viii. 478. 500 copies printed only.

Mr. Tuer has, undoubtedly, by this exhaustive memoir, constituted himself the biographer of Bartolozzi, just as another master-printer, Mr. Blades, enjoys the distinction of being the biographer of Caxton. For many years Mr. Tuer has been collecting Bartolozzian prints, and in these two volumes tells us about them and their author. The illustrations form a noteworthy feature, for they consist of some of Bartolozzi's most characteristic examples, and are printed from the original copperplates in his favourite colours of bistre (or brown), and sanguine (or red). There is not much known about Bartolozzi, but what could be ascertained, Mr. Tuer has very assiduously and industriously collected. Bartolozzi was the son of a goldsmith and worker in filagree ; was born at Florence, in 1727. He showed much precocity in the use of the graver, and in his fifteenth year was placed at the Florentine Academy, there becoming acquainted with Cipriani, the painter. At the age of 18 Bartolozzi was articled to an engraver and printseller at Venice. Shortly after the expiration of his apprenticeship, he married and settled in Rome, working after masters of the Italian school. Returning to Venice, he engraved for patrons and printsellers. In 1764 he was persuaded to come to England by the librarian of George III., and this was the turning-point in his career. He was appointed engraver to the King, and apportioned a salary for three years. The stippled or chalk style of engraving had been introduced just previously. It became "the rage," causing for a time even line-engraving to be neglected. Bartolozzi adopted it, and accepted commissions from the chief printsellers and publishers of the time. In 1769, the Royal Academy was founded, Bartolozzi being one of the original members. He exhibited at the annual exhibition for about thirty years. He made large sums of money easily, but spent them with equal facility. Debt and improvidence following, he was tempted to do inferior work. A contemporary writer speaks of his amazing industry and "philosophic disregard for riches"; his greatness without vanity, and goodness without ostentation. After thirty-eight years' residence in England, in his seventy-fifth year, he left to reside in Portugal by invitation from the Prince Regent. He was there honoured with knighthood and a pension. He engraved very assidu-ously, and died March 7th, 1815, aged 88, almost literally "in harness." Mr. Tuer has done his work conscientiously, and made ample use of the various sources of information available. "Bar-tolozzi and his Works" will always occupy a place in the library of the *amateur d'estampes*, as an almost perfect monograph of the Bartolozzian school of engraving. It had an enormous suc-cess on its appearance, and copies have since been sold at rare prices. A second and smaller-sized edition, in one volume, corrected and considerably added to, has recently made its appearance.

———— The Printers' International Specimen Exchange. Vols. i.-vi., 1880-85. London: 4to.

This is a handsome volume, issued yearly, consisting of specimens of printing. Each member of the "Ex-change" provides about 300 copies of any one piece of work; the entire number is afterwards collated into sets, each contributor thus receiving 300 specimens, all different, in place of his own 300 all alike. The specimens are arranged alphabetically, and Mr. Tuer writes a preface criticising the examples presented and offering suggestions for the future improvement and extension of the plan. The preface and the specimens, with an index, form a volume, issued, as above stated, annually. The idea has received the warm approval of many eminent typographers and biblio-philes. Mr. John Ruskin writes: "I assure you how gladly I hear of an association of printers who will some-times issue work in a form worthy of their own craft, and showing to the uttermost the best of which it is capable." The idea of this scheme was suggested by Mr. Thomas Hailing, a Cheltenham printer, but its practical realisation is entirely due to the energy and enthusiasm of Mr. Andrew W. Tuer, the editor of the *Paper and Printing Trades Journal.* The object in view is the technical education of the working printer, who thus becomes possessed of a knowledge of the progress made by his brethren. Good work and good taste are by this means fostered and mutually encouraged. The beautiful, amazingly elaborate, and many-coloured specimens of which the volume is composed, consist of miscellaneous printing of every con-ceivable description. The "Exchange" numbers in its ranks master-printers, managers, overseers, compositors, press-men, and apprentices. The successive volumes show a marked improvement in the quality of the work, a fact which shows the success of Mr. Tuer's move-ment. He untiringly points out that there is no royal road to the achievement of good printing, and further, that the power—or rather the habit which be-comes a power—of taking infinite pains is the only way to success.

———— Quads, for Authors, Editors, and Devils. London: 1884. 16mo. pp. 94.——Enlarged edition entitled "Quads within Quads," containing a copy of the work in "midget folio."

The contents of the book consist of printers' jokes of English and American origin, and are, many of them, highly amusing. The mechanical get-up is characteristic of Mr. Tuer's originality and humour. The book measures about 6 by 4½ inches. The jokes and *bon mots* fill about one-half of the book, while the other half consists of blank pages fastened together and hollowed out in the middle. In the cavity thus formed is inserted what may be described as a typographical curiosity. It is a micro-scopic copy of "Quads," measuring an inch and a half in length and one inch in width. It is printed in pearl type on hand-made bank-note paper, and consists of 160 pages. The register is perfect and the printing excellent. The "midget" edition, like the larger one, is bound in vellum, has silk strings, and forms a veritable *édition de luxe*. There is something peculiarly quaint in the in-sertion of the one edition inside the other, and when the larger one is closed, there is nothing to indicate the presence of the smaller one within its boards.

MR. ANDREW WHITE TUER was intended for the Church, but finding such a career uncongenial to his tastes, entered one of the London hospitals to study medicine. Disliking this, he went for a short time into a merchant's office in the City, which he forsook for the business of printing and publishing. He is now one of the partners of the firm of Field & Tuer, the well-known proprietors of "The Leadenhall Press," 50, Leadenhall-street, City. Here his restless energies seem to have found congenial employment. Mr. Tuer is the moving spirit of his firm, and it is to him that its great success is mainly due.

It was but natural, that with his antiquarian and artistic tastes, Mr. Tuer should be amongst the first to resuscitate the old style of letterpress printing. His originality, quaintness, and fertility of invention,— not to mention a natural humour of a very pronounced and sometimes irrepressible character,— are apparent in almost everything issued from the Leadenhall Press; so that it is possible to recognise its books by the typographical peculiarities, without reference to the imprints. While some of the books have a uniqueness, and others an eccentricity that is very attractive, all are in thorough good taste. They are interesting and instructive to the printer, for they are never servile copies of something else. Their individual character gives them a value peculiarly their own; while in regard to mechanical execution, they are invariably worthy of the highest commendation. The firm of Field & Tuer confined itself at first to printing only, but when success was assured, the partners launched boldly into publishing. Their art and other books are now known far and wide, and command a large sale. Mr. Tuer has found time for numerous contributions to the leading magazines of the day, besides which he is an author

of some note. His most important work is the beautiful monograph mentioned above, of Bartolozzi. It is dedicated to the Queen. In 1872 Mr. Tuer started the well-known and popular *Paper and Printing Trades Journal*, which he has edited from the initial number, and he has grafted on to it the "Printers' International Specimen Exchange," also cited above. Mr. Tuer seldom puts pen to paper, and the whole of his correspondence and literary work is taken down in shorthand by a private secretary. Mr. Tuer is also a chemist of considerable attainments, and the practical application of his knowledge of the science of chemistry has been attended with useful and profitable results in various directions. After much laborious experimenting he succeeded, some years ago, in producing for the Government greatly improved carbon and manifold papers. These are now largely used in the telegraphic and other services, and are entirely free from any liability to heat spontaneously.

The firm has also published "Journals and Journalism, with a Guide to Literary Beginners," by "John Oldcastle" (pseudonym), 1880, 12mo. It contains notices of several printers and journalists, and a large number of interesting autographs. Mr. Tuer is also the author of "Luxurious Bathing," which has run to six editions. The first was published in folio form, with etchings by Mr. Sutton Sharpe, at three guineas. The last is a most curious typographical production, and illustrated with twelve etchings by Mr. Tristram Ellis. Mr. Tuer's latest book (1885), in its second edition is called "Old London Street Cries and the Cries of To-day." It is illustrated with "Heaps of Quaint Cuts," and has a hand-coloured frontispiece. Of this amusing and covetable book, Mr. Tuer says by way of introduction, "At a guinea in bolder form, the 'Cries' have been sufficiently well received to induce, at the more popular price of a shilling, the publication of this additionally illustrated extension."

TURGAN. Études sur l'Exposition Universelle, 1867. Paris: 1868. Imperial 8vo.

The first twenty-six pages are occupied by an account of the Printing and Stationery departments.

TURIN. Regolamento della Pia Unione de' lavoranti dell' illustre arte Tipografica di Torino. Torino: 1825. 8vo.

——— *See* MANZONI; MAROCCO.

TURRI (Giuseppe). Memorie sull' introduzione della stampa in Reggio d'Emilia e sua Provincia nel secolo xv. Reggio : 1869. 8vo.

TWYN (John). An exact Narrative of the Tryal and Condemnation of John Twyn for Printing and Dispersing of a Treasonable Book, with the Tryals of Thomas Brewster, Bookseller, Simon Dover, Printer, Nathan Brooks, Bookbinder, for printing, publishing, and uttering of seditious, scandalous, and malitious Pamphlets. At Justice Hall, in the Old Bayly, London, the 20th and 22th of February, 166⅗. London 1664. 4to.

Very curious—full of technical information as to the Printing-house of the troublous times following upon the Commonwealth. Twyn was hanged, his head placed on Ludgate, and his body quartered on other gates of the city

TYDEMAN (H. W.). Proeve ter beantwoording van de vraag : " Kan het aan Haarlem met eenigen grond bewist worden, dat de konst, om met enkel verplaatsbare letters te drukken, aldaar voor het jaar 1440 door Laurens Koster is uitgedacht ?—en is niet deze konst van daar naar Mentz overgebracht, en aldaar verbeterd door letters van tin gegoten voor de houten letters in plaats te stellen ? " Dordrecht : 1815. 8vo.

TYNEN (G. van) EN ZONEN. Soorten van Letteren, dewelka benevens vele andere Soorten zoo Hebreeuwsche, Grieksche, Arabische, Syrische, Hoogduitsche, Schwabacher, Latynsche, als Oud-Hollandsche Geschrevene Schriften voor Boeken Kantoorwerken, beneveno allerlei Hoofdletters voor openbare oonkondigingen, alsmede onderscheidene Bloemen en Vignetten. Amsterdam : 1832. 4to.

TYPOGRAPHES et gens de lettres. Paris: 1864. 8vo.--*See* ALONNIER (Décembre).

TYPOGRAPHEUM Luneburgense jubilans. Lüneburg : 1741. Folio.

TYPOGRAPHIA oder die Buchdruckerkunst, eine Erfindung der Deutschen ; bei Gelegenheit der vierten Harlemer Secularfeier zur Ehre dieser Kunst in Erinnerung gebracht. Essen : 1823. 8vo. pp. xii. and 40.

This very ably-written little pamphlet combats the Dutch pretensions to the rights of the invention of printing, and ascribes it to Gutenberg. It is also published in Dutch, translated by G. H. M. Delprat, with the following title :—

TYPOGRAPHIA : of betoog, dat de boekdrukkunst eene uitvinding der Duitschers is ; bij Gehegenheid der viering der vierde Eeuwfeest dier kunst, te Haarlem. Uit het Hoogduitsch, met een opphelderend naschrift van den Nederduitschen Vertaler. Francker : 1823. 8vo.

TYPOGRAPHICAL Album for 1867. Printed by Wm. C. Hutchings, Hartford, Connecticut, U.S.A.

TYPOGRAPHICAL HANDBOOK (The). A Collection of Useful Information and Valuable Tables of Interest to the Apprentice, the Book and Job Printer, the Newspaper Compositor, the Pressman,

&c. ; also Memoranda of Important Events connected with the Art. Compiled by a Practical Printer. Detroit : 1874. 32mo.

TYPOGRAPHIE, La, poëme. Avignon, an xi., 1803. 8vo.

——— *See* PELLETIER.

TYPOGRAPHIIS (de). Earumque initiis et incrementis in regno Poloniæ et magno ducatu Lithuaniæ. Dantisci : 1711. 4to.

TYPOGRAPHY, Invention of.

A comprehensive review of the controversy concerning the origin of Printing has been given in this BIBLIOGRAPHY *s. v.* KOSTER (vol. i. p. 402), and it has been shown that the discussion may be divided into seven epochs, each marked by the appearance of an original treatise on the subject. Since that article was published, the controversy has entered upon another phase, and an eighth epoch has now to be added. The circumstances which have led to this result must here be recorded.

In 1879 the editor of the *Printing Times and Lithographer* obtained the promise of Mr. J. H. Hessels of Cambridge to write for that periodical a review of a new work by Dr. Van der Linde on "Gutenberg." The task was cheerfully undertaken, but its magnitude was not at first realised. Mr. Hessels had hoped that when he had read Dr. Van der Linde's book, professing to be based on documents, he should have obtained all the information he wanted, and should at the same time have been able to lay before the English public—the book was in German—such particulars with regard to this subject as might reasonably be desired. " I regret to say, " Mr. Hessels adds, " that Dr. Van der Linde's work proved to be quite insufficient to meet such a modest demand." Mr. Hessels accordingly undertook an entirely original and independent review of all the evidences in existence which bore upon the question whether Gutenberg can be regarded as the inventor of printing. Mr. Hessels visited different parts of the Continent repeatedly for the special purpose of verifying the deductions of previous writers and examining for himself the various documents upon which they had based their theories.

The result is disquieting if not startling, for it renders almost obsolete even the latest memoirs of the presumed protoprinter. We have given, *s. v.* GUTENBERG, a careful abstract of such facts as have hitherto been accepted concerning him, and probably that article, although necessarily concise, accurately represented the views of the best authorities at the time it was written. Its statements must now be considerably modified, and we can refer with less reserve to its shortcomings, from the fact that in his editorial capacity Mr. Charles Wyman, one of the compilers of the present BIBLIOGRAPHY, was privileged to be instrumental in causing so many historical fallacies to be exposed, through the zeal, industry, and learning of Mr. Hessels.

Up to the present day all that is known concerning John Gutenberg and his connexion with the origin of printing is derived from twenty-three memorials. These consist of manuscripts and relics, and they have all been examined by Mr. Hessels. We have extracted from his work on "Gutenberg" the particulars following. The title of each memorial has been given, or sufficient of it for identification. After that is presented wherever practicable (*a*) a statement as to when, where, and by whom the memorial was originally discovered ; (*b*) by whom and when it was first published, with a reference to the work in which it originally appeared ; (*c*) Mr. Hessels's verdict as to its authenticity or spuriousness, with in some cases his reasons for arriving at his several conclusions. The numbers prefixed are, of course, given merely for convenience of reference ; they are identical with those in the book we epitomise.

We also follow the orthography therein adopted. Nos. 4 to 11 inclusive, with the exception of No. 9, bear upon Gutenberg's proceedings at Strassburg ; Nos. 12 to 23 those at Mentz.

1. A Letter, dated March 24, 1424, written from Strassburg, by Henne Genszfleisch genannt Sorgenloch, to his sister Berthe, a nun in the convent of St. Clara (Reichenklaar), at Mentz.

Published for the first time by Oberlin, in the "Essai d'annales de la vie de Gutenberg," 1801. In 1830, it was declared by Schaab, in the "Erfind. der Buchdruckerkunst," to be one of the forgeries of Professor Bodman, a librarian at Mentz. **Nineteen** overwhelming reasons are **given for** this verdict (p. 11).

2. A Contract, dated Monday, January 16, 1430, with Else zu Gudenberg, Gutenberg's mother, regarding the money which Friele Gensfleisch had to pay her.

In this document, which was found in an account-book of the town of Mentz, is mentioned Henne, son of the blessed Friele Gensefleische. Published for the first time in 1741, by Köhler, "Ehren-Rettung," p. 81, No. 14, Aus dem Schuldbuch der Stadt Mayntz. Hessels believes that the document is now in **the** Town Library of Frankfurt.

3. **A Document, dated Tuesday, March 28, 1430, relating the reconciliation effected through the intervention of the Archbishop, Conrad III., of Mentz and a number of expatriated citizens.**

In this document, Henchin zu Gudenberg is mentioned as "nit inlendig," *i.e.*, as "not being in Mentz." The volume in which it is to be found belongs to the Frankfurt Town Library, but Hessels was unable to examine it. A description has appeared in "Die Chroniken der deutschen Städte vom 16. bis ins **14.** Jahrhundert," bd. xvii. (Mainz), edited **by** C. Hegel. In 1605, the manuscript **was** in the possession of Johann F. F. von Aschaffenburg, and he, or some previous possessor, must have written the date 1581, now seen inside the binding under the title. The contents of the volume embrace the period of 1322-1452, and its chief compiler **was** stated to be "a witness of the **events** which he relates in the latter part **of** his book"; this portion, however, is written in a different handwriting from other **parts** of the book.

4. **An** Act, dated March 14, 1434, **by** which Johann Gensefleisch **der** Jung, genannt Gutenberg, at **the** request of the council of Strassburg, where he resided in the monastery of Arbogast, released Niclause, the secretary of Mentz, and relinquished 310 Rhenish guilders which the town owed him.

Discovered about the middle of the eighteenth century by Joh. Dan. Schoepflin, in a Register of Contracts of the year 1434, preserved at Strassburg. Published for the first time in 1760, in the "Vindiciae Typographiae."

5. A Contract, dated May 30, 1434, with Hengin Gudenberg, son of the blessed Friele Gensfleisch, respecting 14 guilders, which were settled on his brother Friele, residing at Eltvil.

Published for the first **time by Köhler,** "Ehren-Rettung," 1741, **from a manu-**script account-book of the **town of Mentz,** the same volume which **supplied him** with Document 2, *supra*.

6. **A** Document setting forth an action brought, in 1437, by Anna Zu der Isern Thüre, against Gutenberg, for breach of promise of marriage, the end of which affair was not stated in the document.

In 1740, Schoepflin said he received this document from the Strassburg archivist Wencker, along with others. He did not, however, publish the document, whereas he printed all the rest entirely. When Meerman, after the publication of Schoepflin's "Vindiciae," asked for a copy, the latter replied, in 1761, that no such document existed, and that the information in question **was** merely contained in a marginal annotation; and even that was not produced. Hence, Hessels says, the document may safely be considered to be an invention, if not **a** forgery, either of Schoepflin or of Wencker.

7. Six Entries in different parts of three several manuscript registers of the city of Strassburg, containing all that is known of the lawsuit between Jerge (Georg) Dritzehen and Johan von Mentze genant Gutenberg, in 1439.

One copy of depositions of the witnesses, contained in Registers A and B, was found, in 1745, by Jo. Henr. Barth, then archivist, on the clearing out of the Record Tower of Strassburg. The two volumes are stated to have been preserved in the Town Library of Strassburg till 1870, when they are believed to have been destroyed during the bombardment of that city by the Germans. The sentence of the Council, dated December 12, 1439, was written in a third volume, C, which seems to have contained decisions of the Strassburg Council. Mr. Hessels discovered a work by J. F. Lobstein, called "Manuel du Notariat en Alsace," which records that the protocols of 1439, containing the sentence of the senate between Gutenberg and Dritzehen, were burned, November 20, 1793, at a revolutionary fête. All hopes, therefore, of examining the volumes containing the **entries of** this lawsuit have vanished for ever.

In his "Vindiciæ," p. 12, Schoepflin gives a circumstantial account of his alleged discovery of the first section of the document, viz. parts A and B. About 1740 many German and Dutch towns celebrated the memory of the invention of printing; he therefore considered it the proper occasion to investigate it more closely, and began to examine the public documents of all kinds, the commentaries and registers preserved in the Archives of the city, and which were hitherto neglected by his predecessors. Five years after, *i.e.* 1745, the tower called Pfenningthurn, where the Strassburg treasures were preserved, began to be destroyed. He accidentally entered **a** room rarely unlocked before, when, along with H. Barthius, the chief of the archives, **he** discovered a code of 1439, and saw the name of Gutenberg. To Mr. Hessels the story appears suspicious on the face of it. Schoepflin had been very anxious to find a certain date to support his theory that printing was invented **and** practised at Strassburg before Mentz; and this discovery just provided him with one. In his "Alsatia Illustrata," 1761, Schoepflin stated that the remainder, or part C, had been communicated to him by Jac. Wencker, councillor and chief of the public archives at Strassburg. If, therefore, we admit the possibility of the documents having been forged, two dishonest men must have been concerned, as Wencker discovered one part of the lawsuit and Schoepflin another. The reply is, that no one ever saw the sentence of the senate said to have been discovered by Wencker, and that Schoepflin published only in 1760, which was seventeen years after Wencker's death. It may also be said that neither of the two could, if they would, have forged such lengthy documents as those of the Strassburg lawsuit, because in their time people were too ignorant of the language and of paleography. But Schoepflin had unrestricted access to the Strassburg archives, and if he could imitate the handwriting of the 15th century he had merely to take **a** document which contained sentences somewhat similar to those he wished to introduce into his document, to change the names and modify circumstances, and he had all he wanted. Mr. Hessels does not say that this was the case; he merely does not think a forgery impossible. De Laborde examined the entries about 1840, and in his "Débuts de l'Imprimerie à Strasbourg" gives a valuable bibliographical description of the two

volumes A and B. Schoepflin may, however, have found blank leaves in the volumes which enabled him to insert his documents. Dr. Van der Linde, although a stanch supporter, of Gutenberg, is anything but favourable to the genuineness of these documents.

8. An Act, **with** dates, January 12, February **10**, February 18, and March 25, 1441, in which the Knight Luthold von Ramstein and Johannes dictus Gensefleisch alias nuncupatus Gutenberg de Maguntia, both living at Strassburg, remain surety before the judge of the Strassburg cury, for 100 guilders (about 400 fr.) which a certain Joh. Karle, armiger, had borrowed from the St. Thomas Chapter at 5 per cent.

According to Schoepflin this was discovered by Prof. Jo. Geo. Scherz in the Church of St. Thomas, at Strassburg in **1717.** Scherz communicated extracts to **some** friends, who in their turn communicated them to Schellhorn, who mentions them **for** the first time in 1720, in his Amœnitatum Literar., iv. 304. The document was published *in extenso* in 1760 by Schoepflin, in his "Vindiciæ," No. v. The original, according to Schmidt, no longer exists, but a copy has been preserved.

9. A piece of oak, said to be " discovered in Gutenberg's first printing-house at Mentz, im Hofe zum Jungen," on 26th March, 1856, at the digging of a cellar.

This piece of wood is represented as having done service as a press, and bears the inscription—" J. — MCDXLI. — G. N." Van der Linde, who has seen the wood, says that it is evident to the most ignorant that this is an impudent falsification. Mr. Hessels also says that it is regarded by most people as spurious, but he does not himself, not having seen it, feel able to pronounce for or against it. The thing was bought for a very large sum of money by a Dresden gentleman, and is said to be joined to new pieces of wood to form a press, such as Gutenberg is "presumed" to have used. The circumstances under which the piece of oak was discovered have not been accurately described.

10. An Act, dated Nov. 17, 1442, whereby Johannes dictus Gensefleische alias Guttenberg de Maguncia, and Martin Brechter, a citizen of Strassburg, obtain **a** loan of 80 guilders from the **chapter** of St.

Thomas Church at Strassburg, for which they pledge their salvation and Gutenberg's inheritance from Johannes Richter, otherwise Leheymer, the secular judge of the town of Mentz, his grandfather.

This document is at present deposited in the Library of the Protestant Seminary at Strassburg. It was discovered by Prof. J Geo. Scherz, in the archives of the Church of St. Thomas, at Strassburg, in 1717. Published *in extenso* by Schoepflin, in 1760, in the "Vindiciæ" as No. vi. Gutenberg's seal, still intact, is attached to the document, as well as those of the Episcopal Court and of Martin Brechter.

11. Items in the Strassburg Register of the tax of a heller (or penny); in the first of which it is stated that Hans Gutemberg paid a tax in July, 1439, but remained in debt for 12 shillings, which he paid on the 24th June, 1440. He pays again on the 21st September, 1443, and again March 12, 1444.

In the same register appeared No. 6, which was a forgery. The several items were published for the first time in 1760, by Schoepflin ("Vindiciæ," No. 7, p. 40).

12. A Letter relating to a transaction which had taken place 16th October, 1448, and published on the following day, by which Arnolt Gelthuss gives security to Reinhart Brömser and Johann Rodenstein for a loan of 150 guilders, contracted by him in behalf of Henn (Henchin) genssefleisch, called gudenbergk, who now resided at Mentz.

This letter we only know from a later document, dated 1503, in which it is repeated and authenticated. The latter document is preserved in the Town Library at Mentz. Schaab, after he came into possession of the papers of Bodmann—who forged at least three documents in behalf of Gutenberg's biography—published it for the first time in 1830, in the "Gesch. der Erfind. der Buchdr.," ii. 253.

13. A "Notarial document, dated 3 July, 1453, in which Johann Gudenberg is mentioned as a witness, and in which Hans Schumacher von Selgenstadt, brother and servant of the convent of St. Clara, gives to the convent all his possessions," &c.

This note was found among the papers of the well-known Bodmann, but Schaab says (ii. 267) that he has in vain looked for the notarial document or the copy. Hessels says it is a forgery by Bodmann.

14. The Notarial Instrument of the Lawsuit of Johann Fust against Johann (Johan) Guttenberg, alleged to have been decided on the 6th of November, 1455.

This was published for the first time in 1734, by Senckenberg, professor at Giessen, in his "Selector. Jur. et Hist. Anecdot." (Frankf. 1734-1742, 6 vols., 8vo.), tom. i., p. 269. He does not specify the source whence he obtained his documents.

On a transcript of the notarial instrument, which was, in 1736, in the possession of Joh. Christoph. Wolf ("Conspectus," 8vo., Hamburg, 1736), was found written a statement that J. F. Faust von Aschaffenburg is said to have copied about the year 1600 from the original, which was at that time still in the possession of the family, "the instrument of the law-suit of the first inventor of the art of printing, Junckher Johann Guttenbergk, of the family zum Jungen, with Johann Fausten, the first publisher of the said printing-office, about the costs of publishing." This transcript is said to have been among his manuscripts in 1712, and on the 3rd March of that year Joh. Ernest von Glauberg "copies it diligently and correctly." In 1740 J. Christian Wolf, the brother of Christopher, published his "Monumenta Typographica," and gave the notarial document from the transcript which his brother possessed.

Mr. Hessels made a most minute inquiry into the authenticity of this document. He finds that at present all originals are missing, but thinks that it is not impossible that a proper exploration of the German archives and libraries may have unexpected results. There are in existence at Hamburg, in the Town Library, two separate transcripts, made by Von Glauberg from a transcript in a volume containing the Collectanea of J. F. F. von Aschaffenburg, and the Upfenbach transcript, made in 1715 from the "Apographum" of Joh. M. Zum Jungen. At Frankfurt-on-the-Main, in the archives, are the Joh. M. Zum Jungen transcript of the discourse and of the notarial instrument attached to it, made from the "apographum" of Joh. Fr. Faust v. Aschaffenburg. At Frankfurt, in the Town Library, is also a transcript made by Von Glauberg. At Höchst-on-the-Nedder, in Baron von Günderode's library, are several genealogical tables written by Aschaffenburg the elder, in which he distinctly ascribes the invention of printing to Johan Faust, his reputed ancestor. A search has yet to be made for the original register of the Mentz Franciscans, where the trial is said to have taken place in 1455, and which must contain an account of the proceedings, as well as the authentic copies of the notarial instrument, of which three distinct traces are found from 1600 to 1741. Under these circumstances Mr. Hessels does not think it advisable to reprint the instrument from any of the transcripts.

15. An Instrument of the notary Ulrich Helmasberger, dated 21st June, 1457, recording a sale of the property of a certain Dielnhenne, an inhabitant of Bodenheim, to a purchaser called Johannes Gensfleisch, junior. Among the witnesses appears Johannes Gudenberg.

Published for the first time by Steph. Alex. Würdtwein ("Bibliotheca Moguntina," 1789, 4to., p. 229), but according to Schaab with such serious errors that even the Christian name of Gutenberg appears as Petro, whereas the original has Johe. Dr. Wyss, the Darmstadt archivist, says that the original instrument, which is undoubtedly genuine, is preserved in the Mentz Town Library, and has been very inaccurately printed by Schaab.

16. A copy of the Dialogues of Pope Gregory, printed at Strassburg about 1470, by St. Eggestein, preserved in the library of the Earl of Pembroke, at Wilton House, having at the end a fabricated imprint, intended to convey the impression that the book was printed by "Johan Guttenberg, at Strassburg, in the year 1458."

The first notice of this copy appeared in Palmer's "General History of Printing" (London, 1732-1733). The imprint is a palpable forgery.

17. A Document, dated July 20, 1459, representing brothers, called Henne Gensefleisch von Sulgeloch genannt Gudenberg, and Friele Gensfleisch, as relinquishing at the advice of their relatives, Henne, Friele, and Pedermanne, all claims to whatever their sister Hebele had brought with her into the convent Reichenklaren.

In 1830, Schaab ("Erf. der Buchdr.")

says that Fischer (" Beschreib. Typogr." 1800) was the first who made this document known in the German language of the original, from a transcript which he received from Bodmann, who pretended to have discovered it in the archives of the University of Mentz. It was frequently reprinted by later authors, but Schaab declares it to be one of Bodmann's forgeries. Dr. Van der Linde agrees with him.

18. A Letter, dated April 10, 1461, from the Chapter of St. Thomas at Strassburg, to the Secular Court at Rottweil, by which they authorise Michael Rosemberg, the Procurator of the Court, to bring an action against Johann Guttemberg, for the money he owed them.

A copy of this letter was discovered, in 1841, by Professor C. Schmidt, in the archives of the Chapter of St. Thomas of Strassburg, and published by him in the same year, in the "Nouv. Détails sur la Vie de Gutenberg" (8vo., Strasbourg, 1841).

19. Some items in an Account-book of the same Chapter of 1461, in which the expenses are specified which the Chapter incurred through their action taken against Martin Brechter and Gutenberg.

The remarks following No. 18, *supra*, apply also to this account-book.

20. A so-called Rubric, in a "Tractatus de Celebratione Missarum secundum frequentiorem cursum diocesis Maguntinensis."

A copy of this work is said to have been transferred, in 1781, from the Carthusian Monastery, near Mentz, to the University Library of that town. Fischer ("Essai sur les Monumens, Mayence," 1802, p. 81, and "Typogr. Seltenh." 1803, iv. 18) asserts that in this library he discovered it. No one, however, seems to have seen it after Fischer; the book could not be found in 1851 by the then librarian, and, indeed, it was not found up to 1881. But Dr. Wyss has discovered a copy of the work in the Darmstadt Hof Library, but without any rubrics. As a matter of fact, Hessels has proved that the rubric is a forgery, but this time it cannot be ascribed to Bodmann. Fischer says, that he himself discovered the Tractatus with the rubrication.

A very important secondary result has followed the detection of this fraud. It has enabled Mr. Hessels to remove the following **seven books** from the list of works usually ascribed to Gutenberg:—

(*a*.) A Prognostication or Kalendar for the year **1460,** described by Fischer ("Typogr. **Seltenh.**," vi., 69).

(*b*.) Hermani **de Saldis**: Speculum Sacerdotum (*Ibid.*, iv., 14).

(*c*.) Tractatus de celebratione missarum, secundum frequentiorem cursum diocesis Moguntinensis.

(*d*.) German work, treating of the necessity of Councils, and the manner of holding them (Van Praet, "Catalogue," p. 34).

(*e*.) Dyalogus inter Hugonem, Cathonem, et Oliverium, super libertate ecclesiastica (Fischer, "Typogr. Seltenh.," vi., **74**).

(*f*.) Sifridus de **Arena**: Episcopo Cirens.

(*g*.) Sifridus **de Arena**: Responsio.

It may here be mentioned that the discovery **of** one of the initials of the 30-line Indulgence of 1454, in an indulgence **of** 1489, printed by Peter Schoeffer, coupled with other circumstances, has enabled Mr. Hessels to remove from the list of Gutenberg's printed productions also the celebrated 42-line Bible, and the other works in the same type, and to ascribe them **to** Schœffer.

21. A Decree of the Elector Adolph II., dated January 17, 1465, by which he appoints "Johann Gudenberg, on account of his grateful and willing **service**, his servant and courtier **for life**, promising **to** supply him **with** clothing, and each year twenty malter korns, and **two** fuder wines."

Published **by Geo. Chr.** Joannis ("Scriptt. rer. Mogunt.," 1727, iii., p. 424) without **saying** whence he obtained this document. **Later authors** republished it, quoting **Joannis as their** source. Dr. Wyss, however, **has** traced a contemporary transcript **of the** document in the archives at Würzburg. The **text of** Joannis and others are derived from **the** same source, but **are not correct.**

22. An Entry in the Anniversarium **of** the Dominican Church at Mayence, **at** the 2nd February, 1468, which reads:—"Obiit dominus Johannes **zum** Ginsefleis cum duabus candelis super lapidem prope cathedram predicantis habens arma Ginsefleis."

It has been shown **by Dr.** Schenk zu Schweinsberg, the **chief** archivist of

Darmstadt, **that the** entry has no connexion whatever with Joh. **Gutenberg.** *See* his essay, published in "**Archiven des** histor. Vereins für das Grossh. **Hessen**" (vol. **xv.,** p. 337).

23. A Letter of Obligation of Dr. Homery, dated February 25, 1468, by which he acknowledges to have received certain forms, letters, and goods, belonging to the work of printing, which Johann Guttemberg had left after his death.

Published by Geo. Chr. Joannis ("Scriptt. Hist. Mogunt." t. ix., p. 424', without a word as to where he obtained it, and by Köhler ("Ehren-Rettung," 1741, p. 101); the latter adding "ex libro Archiepiscopi Adolfi, p. 80, in Archivo Moguntino." Hessels visited Würzburg to examine the volume in which another transcript of the letter had been discovered. He encountered no reason to suspect the authenticity of the Cartulary in which this transcript is found.

We may now epitomise the results arrived at by Mr. Hessels.

Documents 1, 13, 17.—These are forgeries by Prof. Bodmann, "who had so well posted himself up in the handwriting and language of old documents that he was able to supply his credulous friends with anything they wished."

Documents 2, 3, 4, 5, 8, 10, 11, 12, 15, 18, 19, 21.—These merely establish the fact of Gutenberg's existence.

Document 6.—This is an invention, if not a forgery, either of Schoepflin or of Wencker.

Document (or relic) 9.—This is a palpable fraud, as above stated.

Document 16.—This is a forged imprint, by some person unknown.

Document 20.—This must be a forgery, if it ever has existed at all.

Document 22.—This is not a forgery, but an entry that refers to a man who was dead before 1423, and who was perhaps Gutenberg's granduncle, but not Gutenberg himself.

All the preceding documents are, therefore, either forgeries or they do not help us in the controversy.

Documents 7, 14, 23.—From these Gutenberg may safely be regarded as a Mentz printer, who was established in that city at least as early as 1455; but they leave us in the dark as to whether he was "the inventor," **and as to** what he did print and what **types had** been in his possession.

The conclusion is thus formulated :— "The question 'Was Gutenberg the Inventor of Printing,' I must leave, to my

great regret, unanswered, **because all**
data for a decision are wanting. . . .
As early as Nov. 15, 1454, two printers were
at work at Mentz ; the name of one of
them may have been Johann Gutenberg
(perhaps subsidised by Johann Fust),
but it is not stated anywhere ; the name
of the other is, in all probability Peter
(Schoeffer) de Gernsheim. That the
latter did not consider himself to have
been the first or even the chief printer of
Mentz, seems sufficiently clear from what
we may call his own statement, in the
imprint of the ' Justinianus ' of 24 May,
1458, in which he speaks of two Johannes :
' Librorum insignes prothocaragmatici
quos genuit ambos urbs Maguntina.'
One of these Johannes must have been
Johann Fust ; who was the other?
Everybody says Gutenberg, and I am in
no position to contradict it." That
prothocaragmatici does not necessarily
mean the first (primi) typographers on
earth, we know from the way in which
protho was used in the latter Middle
Ages, it simply signifying chief, principal."

It may be interesting **to** add that the
first distinct mention **of** the name of
Gutenberg, as far as is known, is in a
Chronicle published 14th July, 1474, at
Rome, by Joh. Philippus de Lignamine.
The reference is as follows :—

" Jacobus cognomento Gutenbergo ;
patria Argentinus & quidam alter cui
nomen Fustus imprimendarum litterarum
in membranis cum metallicis formis periti
trecentas cartas quisque eorum per diem
facere innotescunt apud Maguntiam,
Germanie civitatem. Johannes quoque
Mentelinus nuncupatus apud Argentinam
ejusdem provincie civitatem am in
eodem artificio peritus totidem cartas **per**
diem imprimere agnoscitur."

Here, Mr. Hessels points out, is **a**
plain statement that in the summer of 1459
two presses were at work at Mentz, and
one at Strassburg, in the hands of
Gutenberg, Fust, and Mentelin respectively ; but **not** a single **word** is to be
found which **even** touches **upon** the
invention of the art.

It is necessary to **add, that since Mr.**

Hessels's work was issued, and of course,
since this epitome of it was prepared, M.
Claudin, the eminent Paris bookseller,
has called attention to "a new document
on Gutenberg,"—that is, one that has
passed unrecognised till now. It is a
letter of Guillaume Fichet Savoisien,
addressed to Robert Gaguin, and which
is found at the head of some copies of
the " Liber Orthographia," of Gasparini
of Bergamo, printed in 1470. This work,
the preface of which is dated, like the
letter in question, in January, 1470, is
the second which had **been** printed in
Paris, ædibus Sorbonæ, and by the
same workmen who had printed the
first of the letters of the **same author, at**
the end of the year 1469, or **in the first**
months of 1470. In this epistle **to**
Gaguin, written in emphatic but very
incorrect Latin, Fichet says that the new
workmen in books (novum librariorum
genus) came from Germany. Ulric
[Gering], Michel [Friburger], and
Martin [Krantz] affirm that it is a
certain Jean called Bonemontanus
[**Bonne** Montagne, Guten-berg] who
invented the art of printing in the
environs of Mayence. At the time
when these sheets are going to press
M. Claudin's work, in which he will set
forth at length the details of his discovery,
has not been published ; but it is evident
that if the reference is well authenticated,
we have here a supremely important
contribution to the history of typography,
and one that is almost sufficient in itself
to settle the typographic controversy of
the last three centuries. We understand,
however, that the " discovery " is not
regarded as of much importance by men
of such eminence as Mr. Henry Bradshaw, who, it may be mentioned, coincides
with Mr. Hessels as to the " Mazarine "
or " Gutenberg " Bible not being the
work of Gutenberg. Mr. George Bullen,
of the British Museum, read a paper on
M. Claudin's discovery at the Library
Congress at Dublin, 1884, in which he
expressed grave doubts as to its value as
tending to the elucidation of the still
vexed question as to the origin of
typography.

TYPOLOGIE, die Lehre von Abdrucken oder von Buchstaben überhaupt. Hamburg. [n.d.] 8vo.

TYPOMIMOGRAPHIE (la), ou l'art de peindre par l'imitation au
moyen du Calque. Paris: 1830. 8vo.

TYROL. Verzeichniss typographischer Denkmäler aus dem fünfzehnten
Jahrhundert. 2 vols. Brixen : 1789. 4to.

CKERMANN (J. J.). Schriften-Verzeichniss. Erfurt : 1828. 12mo.

UEBER Buchdruckerpresse und Buchdruckmaschinen. In Hulsse's "Maschinen-Encyclopädie," vol. ii., pp. 713-760. Leipzig : 1844.

UEBER den Gebrauch der Freyheit der Presse. Wien : 1781. 8vo.

UEBER die (Wiener) Kaufmannsdiener und Friseure, sammt einem Dialog des Verlassers mit dem Buchdrucker. Wien : [1780?] 8vo.

UEBERSETZUNGEN derjenigen Artikel der k.k. Dekrete, welche die Buchdruckerey und Buchhandel betreffen, etc.; zum Gebrauche der Herren Buchdrucker u. Buchhändler in den Departementen der Elb- und Weser-Mündungen. [Hamburg] : 1811. 4to.

A translation of the sections of the laws concerning printing and publishing, promulgated during the Napoleonic government, at Hamburg and Bremen.

UEBERSICHT der merkwürdigsten u. interessantesten Werke, Bilder u. Kupferstiche, welche am 24. Juni 1840 bei der Jubelfeier der Erfindung des Buchdruckerkunst zur öffentlichen Beschauung ausgestellt wurden. Frankfurt-am-Main : 1840. 8vo. pp. 40.

UFFENBACH (Zacharias Conrad von). De primitiis typographicis, quæ Harlemi in curia et Francofurti in bibliotheca Uffenbachiana adservantur. [In *Amœnitates Literariæ*, vol. ix. p. 969-986.] Lipsiæ : 1728. 8vo.

ZACHARIAS CONRAD VON UFFENBACH was a distinguished magistrate and collector of literary treasures at Frankfurt. He died 1734. He sold a collection of documents to Joh. Christopher Wolf (*see* WOLF, JOH. CHRISTOPH.), some of which have an important bearing on the controversy as to the invention of printing.

UGOLINI (Nicola). Lettere tipografiche al padre Franc. Saverio Laire, autore del saggio istorico della Romana tipografia del secolo XV. Stampate in Magonza nella casa detta Zum-Jungen per l' erede del primo inventore della stampa. 1778. 8vo.

The author's real name was Giambattista [or John Baptist] Audiffredi. This is the satirical attack on Father Laire, author of the " Historical Essay on the Roman Typography of the Fifteenth Century," referred to in this BIBLIOGRAPHY, *ante, s.v.* AUDIFFREDI (J. B.). The work impugned is cited, *s.v.* Laire (F. X.), " Specimen Historicum," &c.

ULLMANN (D. C.). Rede bei dem vierten Säcularfeste der Erfindung der Buchdruckerkunst am 24sten Juni 1840, in der akademischen Aula zu Heidelberg gehalten, von Dr. C. Ullmann. Heidelberg : 1840. 8vo.

ULLMER (Frederick). Specimens of Type and Ornaments. London : 1884. 8vo.

——— Illustrated List of Machinery and Material for Printers, Lithographers, Bookbinders, Stationers, &c. ; also Specimens of Types. London : 1884. 8vo.

Various editions of these trade catalogues have been issued from time to time. Mr. Frederick Ullmer's firm is one of the oldest, in connexion with the printing business, in London. The founder of the house was Mr. Frederick Ullmer, sen., the father of the present proprietor. He commenced business in a small way, in 1825, in Warner-street, Clerkenwell, as a printer's smith, making the iron parts of wooden presses—the Stanhope press at the time very slowly coming into use, and the universally adopted appliance being the "two-pull" wooden press. He made also chases, composing-sticks, &c., one of his best customers being the unfortunate Pouchée, the real inventor of the type-casting machine, although the honour is usually attributed to the American White, whose invention was completed by Bruce. From Warner-street Mr. Ullmer removed to Great Sutton-street, and afterwards to St. John-street-road. In 1845, Mr. Henry Watts, a practical printer, who had just returned from a residence in Italy, joined him, and a removal to the City was decided upon. The new firm of Ullmer & Watts accordingly took premises in Little Britain. This partnership was dissolved in 1852, when Mr. Ullmer took his son into partnership, and began again on his own account in a building, No. 160, Aldersgate-street. He died in 1858, having won the respect and esteem of those acquainted with him. Mr. Frederick Ullmer had removed the previous year to 15, Old Bailey, but in 1875 the premises were found inadequate, and a new building was erected for the business in Cross-street, Farringdon-road, now known as the "Standard" works. Here, not only printers' joinery on a large scale, but machines, presses, and other appliances are manufactured. The business has been a progressive one from the commencement, and the proprietor has well deserved the high character he has attained. Mr. Ullmer possesses a large collection of *ephemerides* relating to printing, files of periodicals, &c., which, especially an extensive series of auctioneers' catalogues, from the year 1846, bound in volumes, might furnish valuable materials for some future history of printing. His trade catalogues are very conveniently arranged, and form useful compendiums of practical information of great value to all interested in printing and the auxiliary arts. In 1884 Mr. Ullmer commenced *The Standard Circular,*—a very useful and interesting quarterly journal, which is posted free to all known Printers in the United Kingdom and Colonies.

ULM. See GUTENBERG-ALBUM zur Erinnerung, &c., *ante, s.v.* GUTENBERG.

Block-books exclusively consisting of texts, without any pictures, either were but seldom made or have been lost, owing to their possessing little attraction. One of the most notable ones known is the Alexander Gallus, Doctrinale, 1446 ; Donatus de octo partibus orationis, Ulm, 1475. There was a guild of printers, including engravers, sculptors, printers, printing was introduced by John Zainer, of blocks, here in 1441. Letterpress as early as 1473.

UMBREIT (A. E.). Die Erfindung der Buchdruckerkunst. Kritische Abhandlungen zur Orientirung auf dem jetzigen Standpunkte der Forschung. Leipzig : 1843. 8vo. pp. xxxiv. 234.—*See* VRIES.

—— Ueber die Ausstellung auf der deutschen Buchhändler-Börse zu Leipzig, während der Feier des Buchdruckerfestes 1840. [In *Serapeum.*] (Leipzig) 1840. pp. 224-236.

UNGAR (K.). Beschreibung der auf der Prager Bibliothek sich befindenden Seltenheiten. Prag : 1786. 8vo.

—— Neue Beiträge zur alten Geschichte der Buchdruckerkunst in Böhmen. Prag : 1795. 4to. [In "Abhandlungen der K. Böhm. Gesellschaft," 1789-91.]

UNGARISCHES MAGAZIN. Band 4, Nr. 26. Etwas von den Buchdruckereyn des 15ᶜᵉⁿ und 16ᵉⁿ Jahrhunderts, &c. Presburg : 1788. 8vo.
A short but well-written summary of the history of Printing.

UNGER (Carl). Flüchtige Blicke auf die letzten vierzig Jahre des vierten Jahrhunderts der Buchdruckerkunst. Berlin : 1840. 8vo.
A pamphlet written on the occasion of the celebration of the quarcentenary of Printing, and containing many interesting facts, most of them based on the personal experience of the author.

UNGER (C. Th.). De Aldi Pii Manutii Romani vita meritisque in rem literatam liber Ungeri singularis. Auctus cura et studio Sam. Lutheri Geret. Vitembergæ : 1753. 4to.
Title-page, dedication, pp. 22 ; portrait of Aldus and plate of his mark, pp. 253. Section I. Biography of Aldus, and account of his printing-office and types. Section II.—Criticisms upon Aldus. Section III.—List of works from his press.

UNGER (Joh. Fried.). Etwas über Buchhandel, Buchdruckerey und den Druck ausserhalb Länder. Berlin : 1788. 4to.

—— Etwas über die Holz- oder Formschneidekunst u. ihren Nutzen für den Buchdrucker. Berlin. [s. n.] 4to.

—— Probe einer neuen Art Deutscher Lettern. Berlin : 1793. 8vo.

—— Prozess des Buchdrucker Unger gegen den Oberkonsistorialrath Zöllner in Censurangelegenheiten wegen eines verbotenen Buchs. Aus den Akten vollständig abgedruckt. Berlin : 1791. 8vo.

—— Sechs Figuren für die Liebhaber der schönen Künste, in Holz geschnitten von Friedrich Gottlieb Unger, dem Jüngeren, Formschneider zu Berlin, und mit einer Abhandlung begleitet, worin etwas von märkischen Formschneidern und in der Mark gedruckten Büchern, in welchen sich Holzschnitte befinden, gesagt wird. Breslau : 1799.

—— Vorschlag, wie Landkarten auf eine sehr wohlfeile Art können gemeinnütziger gemacht werden. Mit einem Versuche, dies durch die Holzschneidekunst zu bewirken. Berlin: 1791. 4to. With a Map.

UNGERER, Zum Andenken an F. K. Heit, Buchdrucker und Buchhändler. Strassburg: 1867. 8vo. 16 leaves.

UNGEWITTER (Christoph.). Dissertationem de variis varietatis librorum impressorum causis, etc. Jenæ: 1711. 4to.

UNITED STATES, Origin of Printing in.—*See* THOMAS.

1487.

UNKNOWN PRINTER.

The name of the printer who used the above device appears to be unknown to all bibliographers. His types are remarkably fine and distinct, and the only book we have met with having his device is " Alphonsus à Spina, Fortalitium fidei contra fidei christianæ hostes" (ff. 248). The device consists of the letters J G, with ornaments, in a border.

UNWIN BROTHERS. A new Biblia Pauperum : being 38 woodcuts illustrating the Life, &c., of Jesus Christ. London : 1877. 4to.

The original blocks were purchased about 30 years since at Nuremberg by the late Mr. Sams, of Darlington. They cannot, it is stated, be recognised as belonging to any printed book, and the artist's mark is unknown to any bibliographer. It is probable that the blocks were thrown aside and never used until about four centuries had elapsed. The book was issued in connexion with the Caxton Celebration, where the original blocks were exhibited. A reduced-size edition of this work was issued in 1884 under the title of "A Smaller Biblia Pauperum."

The founder of the firm of UNWIN BROTHERS, the Gresham Press, near Ludgate-hill Station, was Mr. Jacob Unwin, born 1802, who succeeded to the business of Mr. Robins, of White Lion Court, in Cornhill, in 1826. He afterwards removed to larger premises in St. Peter's-alley, Cornhill, where the present head of the firm, Mr. George Unwin, was born. Another removal was made to Bucklersbury. Jacob Unwin died 1855, and his surviving sons being minors the business was carried on by executors, by whom it was sold to George Unwin. Another removal was made to Oxford-court, Cannon-street, and a fourth change in 1882, when the present extensive buildings were built. Since 1865 the business has been carried on by Mr. George and Mr. Edward Unwin, sons of the founder, under the title of Unwin Brothers. There is a branch establishment at Chilworth in Surrey.

URQUHART (F. W.). Electroplating : a Practical Handbook, including the practice of Electrotyping. London : 1879. 8vo. pp. 216.

Of little practical value as an exposition of the principles of electrotyping for typographic purposes.

────── Electrotyping : a Practical Guide, forming a new and systematic Guide to the reproduction and multiplication of Printing Surfaces and works of Art by the Electro-Deposition of Metals. London : 1881.

The remark on the preceding work applies also to this.

URSIN (G. F.). Bogtrykkerkunstens Opfindelse og Udvikling i 400 Aar. Kjöbenhavn. 1840. Av. pl. cart. 8vo. pp. viii. 96.

UYTWERF (Hermanus). Proef van letteren die gegooten werden en te bekomen zijn, bij Hermanus Uytwerf, tot Amsterdam.

A sheet of large post in the Enschedé collection. The founts are disposed in three columns, with a border running round. There are three of titlings, and six of romans and italics.

────── Vervolg der Proeven van Letteren die gegooten worden, bij Hermanus Uytwerf, t'Amsterdam. [n. d.]

A foolscap-folio sheet in the Enschedé collection. The founts, which are arranged in two columns, consist of the Roman and Italic sizes following :— mediaan, dessendian, and groote garmont. They are all beautifully cut. The sheet contains the following :—" N.B. Alle de bovenstaande Letters zijn nieuw gesneden door J. M. Fleischmann." This foundry appears to have been subsequently carried on under the style of R. C. Alberts and H. Uytwerf (q.v.).

UZANNE (O.). Caprices d'un Bibliophile. Paris : 1878. 8vo. 1 plate, pp. iv. 152.

This most interesting and amusing work contains much information as to typography of a technical character.

ADE-MECUM de l'écrivain, du correcteur, et du compositeur. Lille : 1832. 12mo.

VADE-MECUM für Buchdrucker, Lithographen und Verlags - Buchhändler. Uebersicht und Preise der Illustrations - Reproductions - Methoden, und Schriftgiesserei - Erzeugnisse. (Galvanoplastische Arbeiten, Stereotypen, etc.) Zurich : 1878. 8vo.

Issued by the well-known firm of Orell, Füssli, & Co., of Zurich, chiefly as a guide and pocketbook for their customers.

VALADE (J. J. D.). Notes sur l'ancien imprimeur de la Liste Civile de Louis XVI. Paris : 1822. 8vo.

VALENCIA, printing at.—*See* VILLAROYA.

VALENTINELLI (G.). Bibliografia del Friuli. Venezia : 1861. 8vo.

———— Dei cataloghi a Stampa di Codici. m.s. Venezia : [n.d.]. 8vo.

VALLET DE VIRIVILLE (A.). Les Inventeurs de l'Imprimerie en Allemagne. Paris : 1858. 8vo. pp. 11.
Extracted from the *Revue de Paris* of the 1st February, 1858.

VALSECCHI.—*See* BERNARDI.

VAN BERGEN (Edw.). De eerste muzickdrukkers in Nederland. (From the Antwerp *Vlaamsche Kunstbode* of September, 1880.)

VANDERBORGHT (A. & F.). Fonderie et gravures typographiques. Bruxelles : 1870. 4to.

VANDERHAEGHEN (Ferd.). Bibliographie Gantoise. Recherches sur la vie et les travaux des Imprimeurs de Gand (1483-1850). 7 vols. Gand : 1858-69. 8vo., with facsimiles.—*See also* HAEGHEN, F. Van der.

VAN DER LINDE.—*See* LINDE.

VAN DER PUTTE (Hendrik). Proef van Letteren, die te bekomen zijn by Hendrik van der Putte; op 't Water in de Lootsman t'Amsterdam. [n. d.]

A sheet of post size, in the Enschedé collection. The types, which are arranged in three columns, comprise large initial letters and titling, with Greeks, Hebrews, music and script. To some founts are appended the letters "H. V. D. P." Most of them are identical with those of the first specimen described under Isaac Van der Putte.

Another sheet with the same title in the same collection is large post size. The types are the same as in Isaac Van der Putte's first-named specimen, the initials to the founts being altered to "H. V. D. P." The address in the former has been altered in manuscript to that in the last-named.

There is also a third sheet with a similar heading. Its size is large post. The letters which are in four columns comprise the same founts as before, confined to Roman, Italic, and black. Nearly all of them have "H. V. D. P." appended; but the grootste garmont Roman has "H. Van der Putte inven."

VAN DER PUTTE (Isaac). Proef van Letteren, die te bekomen zijn by Isaac van der Putte; op de Voorburgwal over de Nieuw kerk t'Amsterdam. [n. d.]

A sheet of large post, in the Enschedé collection. The founts are arranged in four columns, and comprise thirty-one of Roman and Italic, three of music, flowers, and one set ornamented initials. The engraving is not very good. To many the initials J. V. P., or I. V. P., or J. U. P. are appended. Another sheet in the same collection, and with the same heading, comprises fifteen founts black, two German, three music, one script, there being the same initials to the founts as in the preceding.

VAN DER STRATEN-PONTHOZ (Comte). Ancien xylographe français. Les Neuf Preux, gravure sur bois du commencement du xvᵉ siècle. (Fragments de l'Hôtel-de-Ville de Metz.) Pau: 1864. 8vo. pp. 56.

A dissertation on the oldest French wood-engraving, previously unknown. This valuable fragment was discovered in the card-board back of an ancient account-book of the Metz Town-hall in the year 1861, the date of the engraving being about 1461.

DELFT: 1477-1487.

VAN DER WEER (Jacob Jacobzoon).

The device of this printer, which is annexed, consists of the lion rampant, holding two shields; on the left one the arms of Delft, on the right one three waterlily leaves. On a scroll behind the head of the lion is the legend: "Delf in Hollant."

Van Dijck (Christoffel). Proeven van Letteren die gesneden zijn door Wylen Christoffel van Dijck, welke te bekomen zijn op de Nieuwe Heere Gracht, over de Plantagie, in de Boekdruckkerij, tot Amsterdam. [n. d.]

A sheet of large post, in the Enschedé collection, with the specimens in four columns. There are twenty specimens of Roman and Italic, with Greeks, Hebrew, blacks, music, and a few flowers at foot. The English pearl was apparently cut purposely for use in Bibles, and the specimen is from the English Bible. All the founts are beautifully engraved, the Italics especially. They were cut by Van Dijck for Elzevir, and the specimen sheet was issued by Athias, whose address is as above. Athias, who was born in 1683, was succeeded by Jan Jacobsz Schipper, whose successors were Wed Clyburg of Amsterdam (1705) and Jan Roman (1767).

——— Proeven van Letteren die gesneden zijn door Wylen Christoffel van Dijck, welke gegooten werden by Jan Bus, ten huyse van Sr. Joseph Athias, woonst in de Swanenburg-straet, tot Amsterdam (*ante*, 1700).

ZWOLL : 1480–1510.

Van Os (Peter).

The above device used by this printer, consists of two shields hanging from a stump, bearing on the right one six printers' balls, and on the left the arms of Zwoll—a cross argent on field sable. This early representation of the inking appliances of the primitive printers is interesting.

Van Praet.—*See* Praet (J. B. van).

Van Weerden (Hugo Janszoen).

The fine device of this printer is on p. 43. It consists of the Eagle, spread, in a Gothic window, holding two blank shields ; above, suspended from the roof, are the cross-keys—the arms of Leyden.

Van Winkle (C. S.). The Printer's Guide ; or, an Introduction to the Art of Printing, including an Essay on Punctuation and Remarks on Orthography. Third edition, with additions and alterations. New York : 1836. 12mo.

Two leaves and historical introduction which commences on page 13 (pp. 1 to 12 are omitted). The technical part begins on page 31, and gives good practical advice, ending on page 236, a plate of readers' marks of corrections following. The first edition was published in New York, 1818.

LEYDEN: 1494-1503. DELFT: 1517.

VAN ZUREN. Officia **Ciceronis**, leeren de walyeghelyck in allen staten behoort te **doen, bescreuen** int Latyn door den. . . . Orator M. T. **Ciceronem,** ende nveerst vertaelt in nederlantscher spraken door Dierick Coornhert, tot Haarlem : 1561. Small 8vo.

In the dedication is the earliest printed claim for Haarlem as the place where printing was invented. Coornhert was an engraver in copper, who associated himself with Van Zuren, who published this book as the first fruits of their new press. The dedication is translated in full in Hessels's "Haarlem Legend," p. 50. The following is an analysis :— 1. Dierick Coornhert had been told that the useful art of printing books was invented first at Haarlem, although in a very crude way. 2. That the art was taken to Mentz by an unfaithful servant, and much improved there. 3. Whereby Mentz, on account of first having spread it, gained a reputation for the invention of the art. Van Zuren does not mention the name of the alleged inventor— indeed, it was not until twenty-seven years afterwards that the name of Koster was brought forward by **Hadrianus** Janius (*See* KOSTER, *ante*).

VARIN (Adolphe). École Liégeois. Les Graveurs, leurs portraits reproduits au burin d'après les originaux. 1366-1850. Avec notes historiques par X. Paris, Liége, Bruxelles : [1882]. -8vo. pp. 137. 36 portraits.

First series of a collection of portraits of artists of the school of Liége, to be followed by portraits of the painters, sculptors, architects, and authors.

VARLOT (L.). Illustrations de l'ancienne imprimerie troyenne. 210 gravures sur bois des xve, xvie, xviie, and xviiie siècles. Troyes : 1850. 4to. 13 leaves.

The pseudonym of Varlot is Varusoltis.

VARRON (De). Les anciens n'ont-ils connu la gravure en taille-douce et l'art d'imprimer des dessins en couleur? (Extrait de la *Revue archéologique.*) Paris : 1848. 8vo. 13 pp.

VARUSOLTIS. Xylographie de l'Imprimerie Troyenne pendant le xve–xviiie siècle. Précédé d'une lettre du Bibliophile Jacob, sur l'histoire de la gravure en bois. Troyes : 1859. 4to.

Consists of 571 original blocks, printed on 72 leaves, on hand-made paper.

VASCHALDE (H.). Établissement de l'Imprimerie dans le Vivarais, illustré de Marques Typographiques. Vienne : 1877. 8vo. Frontispiece and pp. 33.

Extracted from the *Revue du Dauphiné et du Vivarais.* 100 copies only were printed.

VATICAN (The). Alphabetum Grandonico-Malabaricum sive San-scrudonicum. Rome : 1772. 8vo.

Typis Sac. Cong. de Propag. Fide. With an introduction by J C. Amadutius, Præses Typographiæ.

———— Indice de Caratteri, con l' Inventori e Nomi di essi, esistenti nella Stampa Vaticana e Camerale. All' Ill'mo et R'mo Sig. il Sig. Francesco Card. Barberino. Avec une préface d'Andrea Brogiotto. Roma : 1628. 4to.

Title, dedication, and address to the reader, four leaves. Specimens sixty-four pages. A very curious collection of types.

———— *See* ROME.

VAUTHIER (E.). Typographie moderne, ou le véritable Instituteur. Paris : 1816. 12mo.

VAYSSIÈRE (A.). Les commencements de l'Imprimerie à Bourg-en-Bresse. Bourg-en-Bresse : 1878. 8vo. pp. 14.
25 copies printed on Dutch hand-made paper, and numbered by hand.

VEEN (B. W. Van der). De Verbeterde Nederlandsche Letterkast. Tiel : 1852. 8vo.

VEITH (Francis Antony).—*See* ZAPF.

VELDE (J. Van de). Proeve van Letteren waar van de gejusteerde matricen en de vormen daar deselve Letters in gegoten zijn ; als mede den afslag van dien, voor een civile prijs te bekomen zijn t'Amsterdam, by J. Van de Velde, boekverkoper op de Groene Burg-wal aan de oost-zyde in Æschilus.

A sheet of foolscap folio, in the Enschedé collection. The founts, which are disposed in two columns, include six Romans and four Italics, ranging from Augustyn to colonel, with a garmont hooghduyts (a German letter). M. Enschedé has written at foot : " Deeze schriften zyn door R. C. Alberts en M. Uytwerf, of door derzelver voorzaaten gekogt : de tijd wanneer is mij onbekend, dog dit is zeker dat alle deeze schriften nu thans (1768) in de gieterij van de gebroeders Ploos van Amstel bekomelyk zijn." The name of Ploos v. Amstel is placed, in the same handwriting, against each fount.

LOUVAIN : 1473-1477. UTRECHT : 1478-1481. CULEMBERG : 1482-1484.

VELDENER (John).

JOHN VELDENER, whose mark is appended, was a German, probably a pupil of Ulric Zell, of Cologne. He began to print at Louvain in 1473. Like many printers of the Netherlands, he moved his printing-office from place to place. He printed in Utrecht in 1478, in Culemberg 1483. The last book bearing his imprint is dated 1484. In the previous year he printed two copies of the " Speculum " in the Dutch language, and in small quarto form. One edition contained 116 and another 128 illustrations, printed from the woodcuts that had been previously used in the four notable editions. To make these broad woodcuts, which had been designed for pages in folio, serve for pages in quarto, Veldener cut away the architectural frame-work surrounding each illustration, and then sawed each block in two pieces.

John Veldener, as well as his predecessor at Louvain, John of Westphalia, received from the University the honorary title of Master of Printing. He boasted that he was expert in all branches of the graphic arts, but his skill was that of a mechanic. As a publisher he could not compete with John of Westphalia.

VELHAGEN & KLASING in Bielefeld. Haus-Orthographie der Officin, Mai, 1879. 8vo. pp. 8.

—— Ornamenten-Katalog. Eine Sammlung klassischer Buchdruckverzierungen in 3 Alphabeten, in Abdrucken von den Holzschn'tten der Verlagshandlung. Bielefeld und Leipzig : 1878. Large 4to.

VENEDEY (F.). Benjamin Franklin. Ein Lebensbild. 2. Ausgabe. Freiburg i. Br. : 1865. 8vo. pp. 355.

VENICE, printing at. —*See* CASALI, MORELLI.

John de Spira, so called from Spires, the city in which he was born, was the first typographer at Venice. He began in 1469 by the publication of the Letters of Cicero, in types of Roman form. He obtained exclusive rights as a printer from the senate for five years ; but these privileges seem to have been forfeited by his death in 1470. Nicholas Jenson and others went to Venice to profit by the forfeiture, and in 1471 published the "Decor Puellarum," in roman of such an improved form, that he has always had the honour of being regarded as the introducer of the character into Italy. He eventually found that it was necessary, for trading purposes, to relinquish this style and go back to the Gothic letters. He died in 1482. His office ultimately passed into the hands of Aldus Manutius.

VERGIL. Polydori Vergilii Urbinatis, de Rerum Inventoribus, Libri VIII., et de Prodigiis Libri III., cum Indicibus Locupletissimis. Lugd. Batavorum : 1644. 12mo.

Chapter VII. of the second book treats of Books, Libraries, and the Invention of Printing, which is attributed to Gutenberg at Mayence. The engraved title-page bears a full-length figure of Gutenberg with the inscription, "Typographiæ Inventor." Polydore Vergil says, that in 1499, a certain Peter, a German, had invented the art of printing, as he had heard from the latter's countrymen.—*See* VAN DER LINDE, "Gutenberg," page 288 ; HESSELS, "Gutenberg," p. 69.

VERHANDELINGEN van de Maatschappij der Nederlandsche letterkunde te Leydenn. Tweede deels eerste stuk. Te Leyden : 1806-14. 8vo. 2 vols. : vol. i., pp. xviii. 276 ; vol. ii., pp. xlvi. 504.

VERHANDLUNGEN des dritten deutschen Buchdruckertages, abgehalten in Frankfurt am Main, am 9. bis 12. September 1870. Leipzig : 1871. 4to.

—— des vierten deutschen Buchdruckertages, abgehalten in Dresden, am 21. bis 26. Juni 1874. Leipzig : 1874. 4to.

—— des sechsten Delegirtentages der österreich-ungarischen Buchdrucker und Schriftgiesser in Wien, am 1. und 2. November 1873. Wien : 1873. 8vo.

Three reports on the proceedings of delegate-meetings of German and Austrian operative printers.

VER HUELL. (A.). Jacobus Houbraken et son œuvre, avec Supplément. 2 vols. Arnheim : 1875-77. Royal 8vo. 2 portraits.
A detailed description of the engraved works of the famous engraver of portraits, J. Houbraken.

VERI (Lucio). Gli Studi e la Stampa in Roma. (*Nuova Antologia, Giugno,* 1868.)

VERMIGLIOLI (G. B.). Della tipografia Perugina del secolo xv. Lettera di Gio. Battista Vermiglioli al signor dottore Luigi Canali, P. Bibliotecario, professore di fisica nell' università di Perugia e socio dell' accademia delle Scienze di Torino. Presso Carlo Badnuel, Stamp. Cam. e Vesc. Perugia : 1806. 8vo. pp. viii. 209.——Second edition in 1820.

———— Di alcuni libri di rime Italiane rari e rarissimi, pubblicati in Perugia da G. Trivulzio, nel mezzo del xvi° secolo. Perugia : 1821. 8vo.

———— Principi della Stampa in Perugia e suoi progressi per tutto il secolo xv. Perugia : 1820. 8vo. pp. viii. 209.

VERNANGE (Louis). Graveur et fondeur de caractères. Épreuves de Caractères de la Fonderie. Lyon [n.d.] about 1780. Small 8vo., on Dutch paper. 64 leaves.

VERNARECCI (D. A.). Ottaviano de' Petrucci da Fossombrone, inventore dei tipi metallici della musica nel sec. xv. Fossombrone : 8vo. pp. 174.

———— Second edition, with plates. Bologna : 1882. 8vo. pp. 289.

VERNAZZA DI FRENEY (Barone G.). Della tipografia in Alba nel secolo xv. Torino : 1815. 8vo.

———— Della tipografia dei Torrentini in Mondovi. Firenze : 1813. 8vo.

———— Dizionario dei tipografi e dei principali correttori ed intagliatori che operarono negli stati Sardi di Terraferma, e più specialmente in Piemonte sino all' anno 1821. Torino : 1859. 4to. pp. 328.
The work is incomplete. It was stopped after Sav, owing to the death of the author. As far as it goes, however, it is a very useful and important biographical dictionary of the printers of Sardinia.

———— Intorno ai tipografi Fontana. Torino : 1821. 8vo.

———— Lezione sopra la stampa. Cagliari : 1778. 12mo. pp. 37.

———— Appendice del medesimo alla lezione sopra la Stampa. Torino : 1787. 8vo.
Important for the list of printers in Sardinia.

—— Osservazioni sopra gli Annali tipografici del Panzer. Torino :
1793. 8vo.

—— Osservazioni tipografiche sopra libri impressi in Piemonte
nel secolo xv. Bassano : 1807. 8vo. pp. 91.
Biographies of Jean Glim and Christophe Beggiamo, printers, of Piedmont.

VERNIÈRE (Antoine). Note sur le premier livre connu imprimé à
Clermont en 1523. Le Puy-en-Velay : 1883. 8vo. pp. xix.
100 numbered copies privately printed.

VERONA, Printing at.—*See* CAVATTONI and GIULIARI.

VERRONNAIS Châssis servant à lithographier en plusieurs couleurs,
inventé l'année 1844. Metz. 8vo.

VERRONNAIS (Madame Veuve). Épreuves des caractères Français,
Allemands, coulées, rondes, financières, Anglaises, vignettes,
fleurons et passe-partouts de l'imprimerie de Mad. veuve
Verronnais. Metz : 1816. Folio. —— Supplément. Metz :
1824. Folio.

VERSLAG der Commissie tot onderzoek naar het jaar der uitvinding,
en ter ontwerping van een plan voor de viering van een
ceuwfeest der boekdrukkunst. 1822. 8vo. pp. 31.

VERTUE (George). A Description of the Works of the ingenious
delineator and engraver, Wenceslaus Hollar, disposed into classes
of original sorts ; with some account of his life. Second edition,
with additions. London : 1745. 4to.——Second edition, 1759.
4to. pp. vi. 151. Portrait in title, engraved frontispiece and
vignettes.

—— A Catalogue of Engravers who have been born or resided in
England, digested by Horace Walpole, Earl of Orford, from the
MSS. of Mr. George Vertue ; to which is added an account of
the life and works of the latter. London : 1794. 8vo. pp. 238
and 2 leaves of index. Portraits.

The first edition of this valuable work, which has been the basis of all subsequent compilations of the same nature, formed the fifth volume of Walpole's " Anecdotes of Painting in England." Strawberry Hill : 1763. 4to.

GEORGE VERTUE, the engraver and antiquary, was born in London in 1684, and began to practise on his own account in 1709. He was aided by the favour of Sir Godfrey Kneller, and soon made way by his prints. He was one of the first members of the Academy of Painting, established in 1711, and engraver to the Society of Antiquaries. Having pro-

jected a work on the history of the fine arts in England, he undertook extensive researches and collected a large mass of materials, which, after his death, became the property of Horace Walpole, and were published by him under the titles of " Anecdotes of Painting in England," and the " Catalogue of Engravers " cited above. Vertue's prints are very numerous, and among them are a set of twelve portraits of English poets, ten portraits of Charles I. and his friends, and portraits of the Kings of England for Rapin's " History." He was a man of singular piety, modesty, and truthfulness. Died 1756.

VERZEICHNISS einiger in der akadem. Aula am 25.–26. Juni 1840 zur Ansicht aufgestellten, in der hiesigen Universitäts-Bibliothek aufbewahrten alten Druckwerke, nebst einem Verzeichniss Leipziger Buchdrucker von 1480–1500. Leipzig : 1840. 8vo. pp. 14.

—— Typographischer Denkmäler aus dem xv. Jahrhundert ; so sich in der Bibliothek des Chorherrenstiftes des heil. Augustin zu Neustift befinden. Mit 6 Kupfern, 3 Bde. Brixen : 1789–92. 4to. mit Nachtrag.

—— *See also* BESCHREIBUNG ; BILLIG ; DIETRICH (Album) ; FALKENSTEIN ; FLAHTE ; HALTAUS ; KADE ; KUNZE, &c.

VESTER (Christian). Löbliche Buchdruckerkunst. Halle : [1660]. 4to.

A Latin translation by Lud. Klefeker was printed in Wolf's " Monumenta Typographica," part ii., pp. 495–502.

VEUCLIN (E.). L'Imprimerie à Bernay depuis son établissement jusqu'en 1883. Bernay : 1883. 8vo. pp. 33, on hand-made paper.

VICENZA. Catalogo ragionato de' libri stampati in Vicenza e suo territorio nel secolo xv. Vicenza : 1796. 8vo.

—— *See* also FACCIOLI.

[VICTORINO (And. Guil.)]. Typographia Corbolii instituta, ex fastis corboliensibus, octava februarii, latinè, gallicè et metricè. Corbolii : 1799. 16mo. pp. 8.

VIDAL (Léon). Cours de Reproductions industrielles. Exposé des principaux procédés de reproductions graphiques, héliographiques, plastiques, hélioplastiques et galvanoplastiques. Paris : 1879. 8vo. Plates. pp. xxii. 496.

All the different graphic processes are treated by the author ; but special attention is given to the modern ones in which photography receives the largest share of attention.

VIENNA. Beurtheilungen über die k. k. Hof- und Staatsdruckerei in Wien. Wien : 1852. 8vo.

—— Commentatio de primis Vindobonæ Typographis cum variis ad rem litterariam adnotationibus. Vindibonæ : 1764. pp. 48.

—— Das merckwürdige Wien, oder Unterredungen von verschiedenen daselbst befindlichen Merckwürdigkeiten der Natur und Kunst. Franckfurt : 1744. 4to. Numerous plates.

Pages 102–123 are occupied with a "Denkmahl des erstes Druckes," and Plate VIII. is a facsimile of the earliest known block-book.

—— Die Buchschriften des Mittelalters, mit besonderer Berücksichtigung der deutschen, und zwar vom vi. Jahrhundert bis zur
Erfindung der Buchdruckerkunst. Wien: 1852. 8vo. pp.
xxiii. 45 and plates.

A very interesting little work, compiled by a member of the Staff of the State
Printing-office, and showing, by the aid of lithography and typography, the form of
the characters in use from the sixth century down to the time of Gutenberg.

—— Printing at.—*See* AUER, DENIS, KAUTZ, PARIS, SCHIER.

Printing was introduced at Vienna in 1482, by John Winterburg.

—— CO-OPERATIVE PRINTING-OFFICE. First Annual Report of
the Co-operative Printing Office connected with the Union of
Printers and Type-founders of Vienna. Vienna: 1871. 8vo.

This is a co-operative concern, on a somewhat large scale, and one of the very few
of the kind which have achieved a permanent success.

—— Katalog der Bibliothek des Graphischen Club in Wien.
Wien: 1881. 8vo. pp. 24.

—— Specimens of Chromo-Lithography, etc. Executed at the
Imperial Printing Establishment at Vienna, as exhibited at the
Great Exhibition of 1851, seventy fine plates, some executed in
gold and colours, half-russia. 1851. Imp. folio.

—— Specimens of Typography. Executed at the Imperial Establishment at Vienna, consisting of Facsimiles of Manuscripts from
the Sixth Century to the Invention of Printing. The type of the
Gutenberg Bible, Ornamental Letters, Foreign Characters, etc.,
as exhibited at the Great Exhibition of 1851, half-russia. 1851.
Imp. folio.

—— A Survey of all the Objects of the Graphic Branches of Art,
exhibited at the London Exhibition, 1851. London: 1852.
8vo. pp. 16.

—— IMPERIAL PRINTING OFFICE. Alfabete des gesammten
Erdkreises, aus der k. k. Hof- und Staatsdruckerei in Wien.
Wien: 1876. Super-royal 4to. pp. 38.

Some 120 different alphabets, which are alleged to be those of the whole world, are depicted in this book. The Imperial Government Printing Office, where this work was produced, owns all the founts here depicted, some in two or three different sizes. A large number of the matrices of these types were cut at the sole expense of this establishment.

The Imperial Printing-office at Vienna has gained a world-wide celebrity, and attracts multitudes of visitors from all quarters of the globe. In magnitude, diversity of work, and completeness of plant, it has no superior. It occupies five buildings, each from four to six stories in height, and gives employment to over 1,000 persons. There is an interesting account of the place in the American "Encyclopædia of Printing," page 487.

—— *See* AUER.

VIENNET (J. P. G.). Épître aux Chiffoniers sur les crimes de la
Presse. Paris: 1827. 2nd edition. Folio.

VIERING (De). Van het vierde eeuwfeest der boekdrukkunst te
Haarlem, den 10. en 11. Julij, 1823. Haarlem. 8vo. With
plates.

VIETOR (Joh. Lud.). Neu-auffgesetztes Format-Büchlein. Anjetzo
aber übersehen von J. Redinger. (1st edition, 1664.) Frank-
furt-on-Main : 1679. 8vo.

VIETREIUS (Ant.). Brevis excursus de loco, tempore, Auctore et
Inventore Typographiæ. Paris : 1644. 4to.

VIGO (Lion.). Lettera su le Memoire delle tipografie e biblioteche
calabresi del cav. Vito Capialbi, inserita nel Maurolico, an. ii.
vol. iii. Messina : 1839. 8vo. No. 16, pp. 241.

VIGOUROUX (H. de). Hygiène du compositeur typographe. Paris :
1882. 8vo. pp. 14.
Printed for the use of the pupils of the technical school of Chaix & Cie., Paris.

VILLARROYA (Joseph). Dissertacion sobre el origen del nobilisimo
Arte Tipográfico y su Introduccion y uso en la Ciudad de Valencia
de los Edetanos. Valencia : 1796. 8vo. pp. 99, with two
preliminary leaves.

VILLEBICHOT (A. de). Fleuriste et Typographe, ou les apprentis de
la Place du Caire. Operette en un acte. Paris : 1878.

VILLET-COLLIGNON. Appel à tous les imprimeurs de France, sur la
nécessité de demander aux Chambres l'exécution des lois sur
l'Imprimerie et de nouvelles lois réglementaires. Verdun : 1847.
8vo. 4 leaves.

——— L'Imprimerie au xviii⁰ siècle et au xix⁰ siècle, considérée dans
ses rapports avec les divers gouvernements qui se ont succédés en
France, depuis le règlement du 28 févr. 1723, jusqu'à ce jour.
Paris : 1857. 8vo.
The first sheet of 16 pages only was issued.

VILLIERS.—*See* DE VILLIERS.

VINÇARD (B.). L'Art du Typographe, ouvrage utile à MM. les
hommes de lettres, bibliographes et typographes ; contenant, par
chapitres et sommaires, les détails de chacune des deux parties de
cet art, la désignation et les modèles des caractères des langues
mortes et des langues vivantes, les proportions et l'alignement
des vers, un vocabulaire typographique, etc., par B. Vinçard,
Typographiste. Paris : 1806. 8vo. pp. viii. 246, with many
plates, diagrams, specimens, and engraved title-page.

——— Second Edition. Paris : 1823. 8vo. pp. iv. 236, with 8
plates.
The work is entirely mechanical, but well written, and one of the few old manuals
in which there is also treated the question of paper, &c.

—— Idée sur l'origine de l'Imprimerie, ses progrès jusqu'à ce jour et la perfection dont elle est encore susceptible. Paris : [n.d.]. 8vo. pp. 11.

The author describes himself as the inventor of the hamapolygrammatic characters.

VINCENT (J. B.).   Essai sur l'histoire de l'Imprimerie en Belgique, depuis le xve jusqu'à la fin du xviiie siècle.   Bruxelles : 1859. 8vo. pp. 25. ·

Only fifty copies reprinted from the *Bulletin du Bibliophile Belge*, vol. xv.

—— Essai sur l'histoire de l'Imprimerie en Belgique, depuis le 15me jusqu'à la fin du 18me siècle, par J. B. Vincent, correcteur et typographe.   Bruxelles : 1867. 8vo. pp. viii. 223.

Chiefly a compilation, but useful and convenient for its compactness. 350 copies printed.

—— Manuel grammatical à l'usage des compositeurs et typographes. Bruxelles : 1854. 8vo.

A very handy little book, giving the principal rules of French orthography in a plain and easy manner, so that they may really be used with advantage by any compositor as well as the ordinary student of the French language.

—— Manuel grammatical à l'usage des compositeurs-typographes. Méthode de correction indispensable aux typographes, aux éditeurs, et aux personnes qui s'occupent de la correction des épreuves.   Bruxelles : 187-. 8vo.

—— Sur un imprimeur Belge (F. J. Hublon).   Bruxelles : 1857. 8vo.

In *Bul. du Bibl. Belge*, second series, vol. iv., pp. 307-320 with 3 plates.   100 copies only printed.

VINET (Ernest).   Un mot sur l'Alde Manuce de M. Ambroise Firmin-Didot, membre de l'Inst. Fr. Paris : 1875. 8vo. pp. 15.

Extracted from the *Moniteur Universel* of April 21, 1875. 100 copies only printed.

VINGTRINIER (Aimé).   Vieux papiers d'un imprimeur.   Scènes et récits.   Lyon : 1859. 8vo. pp. vii. 408.

VINHOLD (G. A.).   Notis et insignibus typographorum.   *See* ROTH-SCHOLTZ.

VINNE (De).—*See* DE VINNE.

VIRMOND (L. de).   Récréations bibliographiques.   Paris : 1882. 24mo. pp. 186.

VISE (Paul de).   Depositio Cornuti zu Lob und Ehren der edlen Hochlöblichen und Weitberhümbten Freyen Kunst Buchdruckerey. In kurtze Reimen verfasset. Gedruckt im Jahr nach Erfindung der Buchdruckerey 181 [*i.e.* 1621]. 4to. pp. 16.

The only copy known of this rare tract is in the Royal Library, Berlin.   It is the earliest form extant of the printer's "Depositio." (*See* Blades, "Depositio Cornuti Typographici." London : 1885.)

VISSER (Jacques).—*See* MEERMAN.

VITRE (A.).—*See* MENTELIUS.

VLISSINGEN (P. Van). Épreuves d'une première Imprimerie Javanai-e, dont les caractères ont été confectionnés d'après le projet et sous la direction de P. Van Vlissingen, à la fonderie de Jean Enschedé et Fils à Haarlem. Haarlem : 1824. 4to. pp. 22.

In French and Dutch, giving an account of the undertaking and specimens of the new types.

———— Proeven, voortspruitende uit de eerste oprigting eener Javaansche Drukkerij naar het ovaatwerp van P. Van Vlissingen. Haarlem : 1824. 4to.

Twenty-two pages, of which eleven are given to an account of the undertaking, and eleven to the new characters.

VOEGELIN (S.). Christoph Froschauer, erster berühmter Buchdrucker in Zürich, nach seinem Leben und Wirken, nebst Aufsätzen und Briefen von ihm und an ihn. Zürich : 1840. 4to. pp. 24. (Title of wrapper : Zur vierten Säkularfeier der Erfindung der Buchdruckerkunst, den 24. Juni 1840.)

———— Die Holzschneidekunst in Zürich im xvi. Jahrhundert. 1–3. Heft mit Tafeln. [In "Neujahrsblätter der Stadtbibliothek in Zürich" vom Jahre 1879–81.] Zürich : 1879–81. 4to.

VOGEL (E. F.).—*See* SCHMALTZ.

VOISIN (A.). Notes pour servir à l'Histoire de l'Imprimerie dans l'Ancienne Belgique. [Bruxelles : 1850.] 8vo.

Reprinted from the *Bulletin de l'Académie Royale de Bruxelles*, vol. v., No. 10, 1838.

———— Josse Lambert, imprimeur, graveur, poëte et grammairien Gantois du xvie siècle. Second edition, revised and enlarged. Gand : 1842. Royal 8vo. pp. iv. 48. Frontispiece of marks.

Only fifty-three copies printed, all numbered, twelve of them being on fine paper.

———— Notice bibliographique et littéraire sur quelques imprimeries particulières des Pays-Bas. Second edition, revised and enlarged. Gand : 1840. 8vo. pp. 25.

Only forty-five copies printed.

———— Sur Arnaud et Pierre de Keyser, premiers imprimeurs de Gand. [In his "Recherches sur la Bibliothèque de l'Université de Gand." Gand : 1839. 8vo.]

VOLLMER (Hansjerg) (eines Bauern Sohn von Betzingen). Das Buchdrucker-Fest zu Reutlingen, am 24. Juni 1840, beschrieben. (Dialekt-Gedicht.) Reutlingen : 1840. 8vo.

VOLPI.   Annali della Tipografia Volpi-Cominiana colle Notizie
   intorno la Vita e gli Studj de' fratelli Volpi.   Padova : 1809.
   8vo. Portrait, pp. xii. 276.

A complete history of this celebrated Printing-office:

———— Catalogo cronologico di tutte le produzione della stamperia
   Cominiana, dall' anno 1717, fin 'al Maggio, 1756. 8vo.

VOLPI (Gaet.).   La libreria de Volpi e la Stamperia Cominiana,
   illustrate, con utili e curiose Annotazioni.   Avvertenze necessarie
   e profittevoli á Bibliothecarj e agli Amatori de' buoni Libri.
   Padova : 1756. 8vo. Arms of Volpi, pp. xiv. 592 ; pp. xxiv.,
   the last being a catalogue of works published at Padua, and
   dated 1744.

Very rare, only 200 copies having been printed.

VOLPINUS (E.).   De Typographicæ artis abusu, ad studiosam
   juventutem parænesis. Pisis : 1823. 8vo.

VOLTA (L. C.).   Saggio Storico-Critico sulla tipografia Mantovana
   del secolo xv. Vinegia : 1786. 4to.

VONDEL (J. Van).   Grafschrift voor den drukker J. Blaeu. 1763.
   Folio.

VORBERICHT, kurtzer, von einer umständlichen Nachricht, den
   Anfang und Fortgang der Buchdruckerkunst betreffend. Amsterdam : 1740. 8vo.

VORSCHLAG und Entwurf einer allgemeinen Büchermanufactur in und
   vor Deutschland.   Frankfort-on-Maine and Leipzig : 1764.
   8vo.

A satirical essay, proposing to write, print, and publish books, by means of a sort
of joint-stock company, on a wholesale manufacturing scale.

VORSTELLUNG und Bitte der Buchdrucker-Innung zu Leipzig an die
   Hohe II. Kammer der Ständeversammlung des Königr. Sachsen,
   den Entwurf eines Gesetzes, die Angelegenheiten der Presse
   und des Buchhandels betreffend. Vom 18. Februar, 1840. 8vo.

Printed from a manuscript, edited by Dr. Scheliwitz.

VORSTERMAN (Willem).

The device of this celebrated printer is annexed (p. 55). It consists of the double-
headed eagle of the German empire, bearing on its breast a shield with the arms of
the imperial town of Antwerp.

VORTRÄGE, gehalten bei der Jubelfeier der **Erfindung** der Buchdruckerkunst in St. Gallen, den 24. Juni 1840.   St. Gallen
   1840. 8vo. pp. 35.

With an appendix containing a few speeches delivered at the banquet held in the
salon of the Casino.

ANTWERP: 1500-1544.

VOSKENS (Weduwe van D.). Proef van Letteren die te bekomen zijn bij de Weduwe van D. Voskens, letter-snijder en gieter, op de Bloem-graft, tot Amsterdam. [n. d.]

A sheet of foolscap in the Enschedé collection, the letters being displayed in three columns. Including Italics there are thirty-five founts of Roman and Italic, and a note at foot offers all sizes of Greek, Hebrew, Oriental, and blacks. The names of the sizes are :—

Grote canon	Parangon
Cleene (Kleine?) canon	Text
	Augustyn
Canon	Mediaen
Ascendonica	Descendiaen

Garmont	Colnel
Galiard, of groote brevier	Joly
	Engelsche peerel
Brevier	Peerel

There are no means of identifying the date of the publication of this sheet, but it is known that W. Voskens was the proprietor of this foundry in 1677. He was succeeded by "Veuve Dirk Voskens et Fils; Voskens & Clerk (1780); and A. G. Mappa, of Rotterdam."

———— Proef van Letteren die te bekomen zijn bij de Weduwe van Dirck Voskens in sijn leven Letter-Snijder en Gieter, op de Bloem-graft, tot Amsterdam. [n. d.]

A foolscap sheet in the Enschedé collection. The types, which are arranged in three columns, include blacks, Hebrews, Greeks, scripts, and flowers. There are only one fount each of Roman, Italic, and music. The diamond black is very good.

VOSKENS & FILS. Épreuve de Caractères qui se trouvent chez la veuve de Dirk Voskens & Fils, fondeurs de caractères sur le Bloem-graft, à Amsterdam. [n. d.]

A sheet of large-post in the Enschedé collection. The types are arranged in four columns, and comprise forty-five founts all Roman and Italic. To the Groote augustyn, is added "B. Voskens sculpsit"; also to the groote mediaan, which is dated 1707; also to groote garmond, 1705. To the robyn romein is placed the simple date "Ao. 1707." All the founts so noted are very well engraved, though wiry in face. At the end are various figures and contractions, but in none of these Dutch specimens is there a £, which, when required by the English printers, had to be represented by the Italic capital *J* turned upside down.

———— Proben und Abdruck Teutscher Schriften welche zu bekommen seind (bey die Wittwe von Diderich Voskens) und ihren Söhnen, wohnhafftlich auff der Blumengraft in Amsterdam. Allen Buchhändelern und Buchdruckern zu dienstlicher Nachricht. [n. d.]

A foolscap sheet in the Enschedé collection. The founts are in double column, and comprise all the German characters with the following names :—

Gross canon	Tertia oder Bibel
Deyerdank	Gebrochene tertia
Secunda oder text	Grobe mittel
	Mittel

Gemeine mittel	Gemeine corpus oder garmund
Cicero	
Reysander	Petit oder jungfer
Grobe corpus oder garmund	Colonel
	Perl

At the end is the notification "Any kind of punches cut to order and types cast."

VOSKENS & CLERK. Catalogue d'une très célèbre Fonderie de Caractères à imprimer. Cette fonderie, depuis longtemps rassemblée par feu Messrs. Voskens & Clerk, sera vendue à Amsterdam, le 16 Août, 1780, à la Maison du Défunt, sur l'Achterburgwal, au coin du Korte Spinhuissteeg, par les courtiers, etc. Amsterdam : 1780.

The catalogue is preceded by a preface, of which the following is a summary :— "This foundry has long been celebrated throughout the world, and still continues so. Even the English, who seldom praise anything Dutch, acknowledge in their publications that Messrs. Van Dyk and Voskens are great artists in punch-cutting. For instance, P. Luckombe, in 1770, p. 231, praises them highly. We cannot accurately distinguish the punches of Voskens from those of other cutters, but, according to appearance, the majority are from Voskens *père*, rather than Voskens *fils*. We have sometimes been able to verify those of Van Dyk, and have put his name to them. For certain reasons, this foundry is sold in lots instead of a whole, and the lots have been arranged with a view to the convenience of the buyer. The above will be sold without reserve, and with all faults. As far as possible the matrices are lotted with their respective punches, although many matrices are without punches, and many punches without matrices. The gross proceeds of the sale amounted to 8,974 francs; among the purchasers were J. Enschedé & Sons, Ploos van Amstel, Treiter, Posthumus, De Bruyn, and De Groot."

———— Épreuve de caractères qui se trouvent chez Voskens et Clerk. [n. d.]

A sheet, like the last, in the Enschedé collection, with the foot-note in French.

———— Proef van Letteren, &c., die te bekomen zijn * * * letter-gieter of de Oude zijds agter Burghwal, tot Amsterdam. [n. d.]

A royal sheet in the Enschedé collection printed as two folio pages, each having a heading as above. The first folio is devoted to blacks, music, and scripts, and the second to titling letters and flowers. To the paragon duyts is added " Gesn. door B. Voskens " ; to the mediaan duyts, "Gesn. door B. Voskens, 1710 " ; to the descendiaan, "Gesn. door B. Voskens " ; also to the groote augustyn noten and to the descendiaan noten. The largest capitals on the second folio are described as " op hout gesneden " (cut in wood).

———— Proef van Letteren die te bekomen zijn, bij Voskens en Clerk. [n.d.]

A large sheet royal, in the Enschedé collection. It is the same as that described under Voskens & Fils, with the head altered. At foot is " Nog zyn t'Amsterdam op de Agter burgwal, over 't Prince-hof; by dezelve te bekomen, Haerlemische."

VRIES (Dr. A. de). Bewijsgronden der duitschers voor hunne aanspraak op de uitvinding der boekdrukkunst, of beoordeeling van het werk van A. E. Umbreit ; "die Erfindung der Buch-druckerkunst." 'sGravenhage : 1844. 8vo. pp. xvi. 208. 3 pages of Greek verse.

———— Argumens des Allemands en faveur de leur prétention à l'Invention de l'Imprimerie, ou examen critique de l'ouvrage de M. A. E. Umbreit : Die Erfindung, &c. traduit du hollandais par J. J. F. Noordziek. La Haye : 1845. Royal 8vo. pp. xxxiv. 212.

———— Beschrijv. van twee prachtexemplaren der 8 folio afdruken van de Fransche vertaling d. werken over de uitvinding d. boek-drukkunst. 'sGravenhage : 1828. 8vo.

[————] Bewijzen voor de echtheid en gelijkenis der oude afbeeldingen van Coster. Ter wederlegging van het van Iets van den heer Van Westreenen. Haarlem : 1847. 8vo.

VOL. III.   I

[———] Bijdragen tot de Geschiedenis der Uitvinding van de Boekdrukkunst. Haarlem : 1823. 8vo.
Privately printed.

——— Boekdrukkunst (overgenommen uit den Algemeenen Konst-
en Letterbode. 1841. N. 52). Large 8vo. pp. 10.

——— Brief aan A. D. Schinkel over Guichard's Notice sur le
Speculum humanæ salvationis, met drie bijlagen tot staving der
naauwkeurigheid van het verhaal van Junius wegens de uitvinding
der boekdrukkunst en ter wederlegging der meening : dat Coster,
koster zou geweest zijn. 'sGravenhage : 1841. 8vo. pp. xii.
144.

——— Eclaircissemens sur l'histoire de l'invention de l'Imprimerie
contenant : Lettre à M. A. D. Schinkel, ou réponse à la notice de
M. Guichard sur le Speculum Humanæ Salvationis. Dissertation
sur le nom- de Coster et sur sa prétendue charge de sacristain.
Recherches fait à l'occasion de la quatrième fête séculaire à
Haarlem en 1823. Traduit du hollandais par J. J. F.
Noordziek. La Haye : 1843. 8vo. pp. xlii. 275.

[———] Hedendaagsche voorstelling van Coster en de uitvinding der
boekdrukkunst, in Frankrijk. 'sGravenhage : 1853. 8vo. pp.
iv. 31.

——— Lijst der stukken betrekkelijk de geschiedenis van de
uitvinding der boekdrukkunst berustende op het raadhuis te
Haarlem. Haarlem : 1862. 8vo. Large 4to. pp. iv. 50.

[———] Lotgevallen van Coster's woning. Haarlem : 1851. 8vo.
pp. 40.
An account of De Vries and an outline of his theories will be found, *ante*,
s.v. KOSTER.

VUY (Jules).   Imprimeur et libraire de Savoie.   Notes bibliographiques.   Annecy : 1878.   8vo.   pp. 30.
Extracted from the *Revue Savoienne*, November, 1877.

(C.) John Gutenberg: a Romance.
London: 1860. 4to.

WAAGEN (Dr. Gustav Friedrich).
Galleries and Cabinets of Art
in Great Britain. London: 1857.
8vo.

Account of the Block books.

———— Treasures of Art in Great
Britain. London: 1854. 8vo.

Account of the Block books.

WACKERNAGEL (Rudolf). Rechnungsbuch der Froben und
Episcopius, Buchdrucker und Buchhändler zu Basel, 1557-64.
Basel: 1881. 8vo. pp. vii. 150.

A very curious book, being the debtor and creditor account between the
famous printer Froben and the Bookseller Episcopius, for seven years.

WADSKIÆR (Christian Friderik). Det Kongelig Privilegerede
Nörre-Jyllandske Bogtrykkeries förste Pröve, eller nogle Linea-
menter af Bogtrykker-Konstens Historie i Dannemark. Wiborg:
1738. 4to.

The author tries to prove that Nicolas Jenson was a Dane, and the inventor of
printing.

———— Gedancken von dem ersten Erfinder der Buchdruckerkunst,
aus dem Dänischen übersetzt, mit C. F. Gessner's Anmerkungen.
[In Gessner's "Buchdruckerkunst und Schriftgiesserey," part iii.,
p. 93, et seq. Leipzig: 1719. 8vo.]

WAGNER (Johannes Rudolph). Hand- und Lehrbuch der Technologie.
Five vols. Leipzig: 1862. 8vo.

The subject of vol. iv. is Printing.

WAGNER (Wilhelm). Die drei Tage der Enthüllungsfeier des Gutenberg-Monuments am 14., 15. und 16. August 1837. Aufgefasst
von einem Frankfurter Typographen. Mit Vorwort, vollständigen
Festreden und Anhang. Zum Besten des Gutenberg-Monuments
hrsg. von Heller & Rohm, Buchdruckern in Frankfurt-am-Main.
Frankfurt-am-Main : 1837.   8vo.

WAINHOUSE (Abraham). Trades Unions justified by Facts and re-
putable Authorities ; with practical Suggestions to Operative
Printers as to the Mode of securing a Portion of the Benefits
arising out of the Abolition of the Paper Duty. Manchester : 1861.
This essay gained the prize of £5 offered in 1861 by the executive of the Provincial
Typographical Association.

WAIT. A New Printing Press.   *Gentleman's Magazine*, lxxxi.,
part 2, p. 576.

A description, dated Dec. 1811, of a newly-invented printing-press which had been constructed at Philadelphia, U.S., by Mr. Wait. Distribution of the ink over the types as well as the printing was performed by cylinders, which, with the tympan and frisket, were all operated by machinery to which motion was given by horse, steam, or water power. The same power could work several presses, the only attention necessary being that of a lad at each press, to place and remove the sheets.

WALCKENAER (C. A.). Lettres sur les Contes des Fées.   Paris :
1862.   8vo.
Contains memoir of Daunou.

WALDAU (Georg Ernst). Leben Anton Koburgers, eines der ersten
und berühmtesten Buchdruckers in Nürnberg, nebst einem Verzeichnisse aller von ihm gedruckten Schriften. Dresden und
Leipzig : 1786.   8vo.   Three preliminary leaves.   pp. 42.

WALDHECKER. Die Kunst einen gleichförmigen Druck bei Stein-
druck zu erreichen. Osnabrück : 1832.   8vo.

WALDOW (Alexander). Anleitung zum Satz und Druck von Aktien.
Leipzig : 1875.   4to.   pp. 52.
Some valuable instructions on the tasteful composition of shares, coupons, &c., is
here afforded.

———— Anleitung zum Zeichnen von Correcturen auf Druckarbeiten,
nebst Erklärung typograph. Fachausdrücke und Belehrung über
die Herstellung von Druckwerken. Leipzig : 1873. 8vo.————
Second edition. Leipzig : 1878.   8vo.
A dissertation on printers' corrections, technical terms, &c., specially intended for
the use of proof-readers, authors, publishers, &c.

———— Die Buchdruckerkunst über die verwandten Geschäftszweige.
Leipzig : [1871].   4to.   With plates and woodcuts.

—— Die Buchdruckerkunst in ihrem technischen und kaufmännischen Betriebe. Vol. i. vom Satz; Vol. ii. vom Druck. Leipzig: **1874.** 4to. With Atlas of 109 plates of Printing-presses.

A very comprehensive work on Typography. The first volume treats on composition, &c., while the second volume is devoted to press and machine-printing. The work is profusely illustrated.

—— Hülfs-Büchlein für Buchdrucker und Schriftsetzer, sowie für Factoren, **Correctoren** und **Verlagsbuchhändler.** Leipzig: 1872. 12mo.

—— Kurzer Rathgeber für die Behandlung der Farben bei Ausführung von Bunt- u. Tondrucken, Bronce-, Blattgold- u. Prägedrucken auf der Buchdruckpresse und Maschine. Leipzig: 1868. 8vo. **pp. 32.**——Third edition. Leipzig 1884. **8vo.** A good practical work.

—— Die Lehre vom Accidenz-Satz. Leipzig: 1875. 4to.

—— Lehrbuch für Schriftsetzer. Leipzig: **1877.** Royal 8vo.

This "Guide to Jobbing Printing" is a reprint of a portion of the first volume of "Die Buchdruckerkunst in ihrem technischen und kaufmännischen Betriebe," and gives some valuable instruction on the subject of job printing, with 69 illustrations.

—— Die Schnellpresse und ihre Behandlung vor und bei dem Drucke. Leipzig: 1872. 4to. pp. 94. 36 illustrations.

A machine-minder's practical guide, reprinted from the *Archiv für Buchdruckerkunst*, and intended as a companion volume to Eisenmann's "Guide on Printing-machine Construction," &c.—*See* EISENMANN (A.).

—— Die Zurichtung und der **Druck von Illustrationen.** Kurzer Leitfaden für Maschinenmeister. Separatabdruck aus dem *Archiv für Buchdruckerkunst.* Leipzig: **1867.** 4to. pp. 59. Nine plates.

An illustrated manual on the making-ready and printing of woodcuts, &c.

—— Second Edition. Leipzig: 1879. 4to. pp. 40, frontispiece, and 14 plates.

This treatise on the art of making-ready and printing wood-cuts has the rare merit of illustrating in its general get-up what is theoretically enjoined in the text. Composition, press-work, paper, and binding, are severally made to contribute their share to the completion of this elegant book. The work opens with a lucid historical sketch of the invention and gradual progress of the art of wood-engraving, and the several chemico-typographic processes which have been introduced in recent times, come in for a brief share of attention. The practical part of the work begins with some remarks on the wetting of paper. The instructions under this head are explicit, and it is pointed out that should paper continue stiff and hard, even after wetting, the addition of a small quantity of glycerine to the water is sure to remedy this defect. The rules to be observed with regard to the rolling of paper, the description of ink to be used in printing, the fixing of the form on the press or machine, the quality of the printing-rollers, &c., are severally dealt with in separate chapters, and the information on each point is eminently practical.

The actual process of "making-ready," and all that it implies as to overlays, underlays, &c., is next elucidated, and a number of separate illustrations demonstrate, even to the veriest tyro at press or machine, the different aspect presented by the rough impressions of a cut, and its finished appearance after the finer and middle tones have been duly brought up. The book closes with some useful wrinkles on the printing of tint plates, and an exposition of the processes followed in the production of the fourteen sheets of illustrations which form a kind of appendix. In addition to a variety of woodcut impressions, there are also a series of illustrations produced by photo-lithography, photo-zincotype, zinc etching in relief (Leitch's process), graphotype, chemitype. Dallastype, and heliography. The whole work reflects the greatest credit upon Herr Waldow, its author, printer, and publisher, the fame of whose press this book will help to enhance.

―――― The Festival Days of the Printer. Leipzig : 1858. 8vo.

This is a neat little volume in German containing recitations, songs, toasts, &c., appropriate for festivals and meetings of the Craft.

―――― Anleitung zum Farbendruck auf der Buchdruckpresse und Maschine. Mit Berücksichtigung des Iris- Bronze- und Blattgolddrucks. Leipzig : 1883. Royal 8vo. Title printed in gold and colours, and two supplements, giving twenty-eight specimens of colour-printing.

―――― Winke über die Preisberechnung von Druckarbeiten. Leipzig 1884. 8vo.

―――― Die Tiegeldruckmaschine, ihre Konstruction und Behandlung vor und während des Druckes. Ein Leitfaden für Buchdrucker und Laien. Leipzig : 1880. 12mo. Numerous illustrations.

―――― Taschen-Agenda für Buchdrucker. Schreib-, Merk- und Notiz-Kalender. Leipzig : 1876. 8vo.

―――― Illustrierte Encyklopädie der Graphischen Künste, und der verwandten zweige-buch-stein-und kupferdruck, lithographie, photolithographie, chemitypie, zinkographie, xylographie, schriftgiesserei, stereotypie, galvanoplastik, &c. Leipzig : 1884. Lar. 8vo. pp. x. 911.

This is incomparably the best and most complete encyclopædia of printing and the correlated arts that has ever appeared. It is a monument of industry and technical erudition. There are no less than 2,798 articles, 581 illustrations, and two plates. Herr Waldow acted as editor, being assisted by ten or more authorities on special subjects. The machinery and processes of all countries are described and illustrated, and there are memoirs and portraits of the most noted persons who have been connected with printing.

WALFORD (Cornelius). Printing Patents. [Two articles in the *Bibliographer*, October and November, 1884. London : 1884. 4to.]

WALKER (S.). The Road: Leaves from the Sketch-Book of a Commercial-Traveller. By the "Whistling Commercial." Otley: 1872. 8vo.

This is an amusing book of travelling reminiscences, written by Mr. S. Walker, of the Yorkshire Printing and Publishing Company, and includes several sketches of printers, publishers, and booksellers.

WALL (A. H.). Art Illustration. A History and Practical Guide for Authors, Printers, Publishers, and Artists engaged in the production of Illustrated Books and Periodicals. London : 1878. 8vo. pp. 16.

WALLACE (John William). An Address, delivered at the Celebration by the New York Historical Society, May 20, 1863, of the **Two** Hundredth Birthday of Mr. William Bradford, who introduced the Art of Printing into the middle Colonies of British America. Albany : 1863. 8vo. pp. 114. Two preliminary leaves.

The first printer to **the** middle colonies of America was William Bradford, who came from England in 1682, with William Penn, and settled in Philadelphia before that city was laid out, where he had a printing-press as early as 1686. In 1692 he was induced to remove to New York, where he was also the first printer. He died in 1752, aged 92. His monument is in Trinity churchyard, New York. He established the first newspaper in Philadelphia, and also the first paper in New York. In the year 1863 there was a celebration of his 200th birthday by the New York Historical Society, when his monument was restored, with the original inscription. It will be observed that the dates are somewhat discordant.

———— Early Printing in Philadelphia. In *Pennsylvania Magazine of History*, No. 16. Philadelphia. 8vo.

Gives some curious information about the Friends' Press, which was established in the interval between William Bradford, the first printer of Philadelphia, and the second Bradford.

———— An Old Philadelphian. Col. William Bradford, the Patriot Printer of 1776. Sketches of his Life. Philadelphia : 1883. 8vo. pp. 517. Privately printed.

Contains an exhaustive catalogue of the books printed by the Bradfords, the pioneer printers of the United States.

WALLMARK (P. A.). Johan Gutenberg. Hans Uppfinning, dess Utbredande och Framsteg. Historiskt Utkast i Anledning af Boktryckerikonstens fjerde Jubel-år ; uppläst vid deni Frimurare-Ordenslokal af Boktryckeri-Societeten föranstaltade Fest, den 5. Juli 1840. Stockholm : 1840. 4to. pp. 114. Plate of Gutenberg's statue at Mayence.

On pp. 39 to 43 and on pp. 54 to 64 appear sundry notes about the printing-offices of Sweden, which, however, do not impart anything new.

WALPOLE (Horace).—*See* STRAWBERRY HILL, and VERTUE (Geo.).

WALTER (F). Bildung und Halbbildung. Ein Sendschreiben an die Gebildeten des Preussischen Volkes bei Gelegenhist der Thronbesteigung Friedrich Wilhelm IV. und des Gutenbergfestes in Berlin. Berlin : 1840. 8vo. pp. 31.

WALTER (John). An Address to the Public, showing the great Improvement he has made in the Art of Printing by Logographic Arrangements ; stating also the various Difficulties and Oppositions he has encountered during its progress, to the present state of perfection. London : 1789. 8vo.

———— Miscellanies in Prose and Verse, intended as a Specimen of the Types at the Logographic Printing Office. London : 1785.

The first twelve pages of the Introduction consist of a letter signed J. Walter, deprecating the opposition which the system of logographic types had to contend with from " selfish printers and false friends." The volume forms a good specimen of printers' work, the type ranging from pica at the commencement to nonpareil at the end of the book.

—— Three Letters headed thus :—"Mr. Walter having been informed that a number of illiberal reports in various shapes are circulated to the prejudice of his Press, some of them going so far as to annihilate its continuance, has thought it right to lay before the public the following letters which were published in the *Daily Universal Register*, of the 10th, 11th, and 12th of August last (17—), which he submits to candid inspection." 4 pp. folio, small type. London : 17—.

Occupied entirely with an account of the opposition the Logographic system had met with. At the end is a list of forty books printed logographically, and an announcement that the "Logographic Founts and Types may be seen at the British Museum, to which place a Fount has been removed from the Queen's Palace." By this process, says the author, "the Errors are far less than in common, and there can be none orthographical, *nor any misplacing or substitution of one letter for another.*" It is curious after reading this to notice upon the title-page *N*agesty instead of *M*ajesty. "The total number of pieces required is not much above 3,500." "This vast quantity of Types and extent of space does not in the least retard the compositor."

WALTER PRESS (The). Reprinted from the *Scotsman.* London : 1872. 32mo. pp. 25.

The "Walter" Press, which has superseded the Hoe Machine (which see), is the joint invention of Mr. J. C. Macdonald, the manager of the *Times* Printing Establishment, and Mr. J. C. Calverley, the chief engineer there. It was introduced in 1869, and named after Mr. John Walter, M.P., the principal proprietor of the leading journal. His father and namesake was the first to print a newspaper by steam-power in 1814. His grandfather, also of the same name, was the originator of the *Times.*— *See* PATENT OFFICE PUBLICATIONS.

—— The Walter Press. Reprints of descriptions from the *Scotsman*, the *New York Times, Macmillan's Magazine,* and the *Printers' Register.* London : 1876. 16mo. pp. 40.

—— *See* SMILES.

The founder of the Walter family, identified for several generations with the history of the "leading journal," was John Walter, a Newcastle coalbuyer, who died in 1755. His son, John Walter the second, was born in 1738 ; died 16 November, 1812, aged 74. He also was a coal-merchant, and an underwriter. When on the high road to fortune he was nearly ruined by a fleet of merchantmen, on which he had taken a large risk, being captured by the French. In 1782, he became acquainted with Henry Johnson (*q.v.ante*), the author of the "Introduction to Logography." Johnson made what he considered great improvements in the art of printing, and Mr. Walter being impressed with those improvements, assisted to complete them. In 1784, he took the premises then vacant in Printing House-square, where, in 1666, John Bill had founded and printed the *London Gazette.* The monastery of the Black Friars formerly occupied that site : the office of the *Times* now stands there. Mr. Walter laboured hard and successfully to qualify himself for the printing business, in which he had embarked as a mere novice ; hence, "want of experience laid him open to many and gross impositions." He founded the newspaper now known as the *Times,* to prove that newspapers as well as books could be printed far better and more cheaply than by the system in common use. A large number of books issued from his logographic press, but the system had to be abandoned at last. His journal, started 1st January, 1785, was called the *Daily Universal Register,* being changed to the *Times* on 1st January, 1788. He had to undergo many harassing and costly actions for libel, and was actually committed to Newgate. He was about relinquishing his paper, but thought better of it, and associated his son in its management.

This son, John Walter the third, was born in 1776, educated at Merchant

Taylors' School, and studied at Oxford. He was afterwards regularly apprenticed to his father, and mastered the art of printing. He was twenty-seven when he undertook the sole management of the *Times*, and this was the beginning of its prosperity and the source of its fame. He found it a struggling and feeble journal, he left it the most successful and powerful journal in the world. On the death of his father, he became sole proprietor. He made several attempts to effect improvements in the printing-press. He consulted Marc Isambard Brunel, one of the great mechanics of the day, who gave his best attention to the matter, and then intimated his inability to execute what was required. Mr. Walter advanced money to Thomas Martyn, who thought he had made an important discovery, but his ideas were not practicable. It was while engaged in seeking for a person who could give scope and effect to his wishes, that he was introduced to Frederick Koenig, who was also labouring to effect improvements in the printing-press (*see* GOEBEL). An account of Koenig will be found in the work,—not published when the early part of this BIBLIOGRAPHY was compiled,—"Friederich Koenig und die Erfindung der Schnellpress. Ein biographisches denkmall." Large 4to., pp. viii. and 280 ; plates. Stuttgart, 1883. The author is M. Theo. Goebel. An elaborate reply to this work was published in the *Printers' Register*, under the heading "The Invention of the Steam Press," from October, 1883, to June, 1884 (vol. xxiii.). The author is Mr. William Blades. Mr. Goebel has compiled a rejoinder, the first instalment of which appears in the same periodical, March, 1885.

From the date of the *Times* being printed by steam down to the present day, unceasing efforts have been made with a view to perfect machinery in that office. Mr. Walter died in 1847, aged 74. He had sat in Parliament as member for Berkshire and for Nottingham. He acquired much wealth as well as fame. The present Mr. John Walter is the fourth of the name in direct lineal succession. He has been the instigator of great improvements in printing and journalism. He first induced Applegath to improve on Koenig's press (*see* APPLE-GATH, *ante*); then Applegath and Cowper invented another press. Afterwards ten-cylinder Hoe machines were introduced (*see* HOE, *ante*). Meantime, he encouraged Dellagana to prosecute his experiments in producing stereo plates by the papier-mâché process. This method was adopted in the *Times* office in 1850. Finally, he was instrumental in producing the "Walter Press," patented between 1863 and 1871, by Mr. John Cameron MacDonald, the present practical manager of the establishment, and Mr. Joseph Calverley, engineer. The publications cited above give an account of this machine. Mr. Walter has also had the composing-machine invented by Kadenheim greatly improved ; it now sets up the most of the news portion of the *Times*. Many interesting details concerning the Walter family will be found in an article headed "The Centenary of the *Times*," by Mr. Fraser Rae, in the *Nineteenth Century* for January, 1885 (vol. xvii. pp. 43-65).

WALTHER (Christophorus). Antwort auff Sigmund Feyerabends und seiner Mitgesellschafft falsches Angeben und Lügen, so in nehest vergangener Herbst Messe des 1570. Jars., zu Franckford am Meien ist ausgangen. Wittemberg : 1571. 4to. pp. 48. (Neither the leaves nor the pages are numbered.)

The author was a reader in the office of Hans Lufft, the Bible-printer of Dr. Martin Luther; the pamphlet is directed against the Francfort Bible-printer Feyerabend, who had reprinted, without permission, the Lutheran translation first printed by Lufft.

WALTHER (Dr. C. F.). Catalogue Méthodique des dissertations ou thèses académiques imprimées par les Elzevir de 1616-1712, recueillies pour la première fois dans la Bibliothèque publique à St. Pétersbourg. Supplément aux Annales de l'Imprimerie des Elzevir, publiée par M. Charles Pieters, à Gand. Bruxelles : 1864. 8vo. pp. 107.

—— Les Elzevir de la Bibliothèque Impériale publique de St. Pétersbourg. Catalogue Bibliographique et Raisonné, publié sous les auspices et aux frais du Prince Youssoupoff. St. Pétersburg : 1864. Sq. J2mo. pp. xxiv. 332.

Bibliographical and Typographical annotations throughout.

—— Beiträge zur Kenntniss der Hofbibliothek zu Darmstadt. Darmstadt : 1867. 8vo.

Contains an important reference to a Prognostication or Calendar said to be for 1460, and therefore printed 1459, described by Fischer (Typogr. Selleuh. vi., 69). Referred to by Hessels, "Gutenberg," p. 108.

WALTHER (K.). Gedicht zum Festmahle des Jubiläums der Buchdruckerkunst in Göttingen den 24. Juni 1840. Göttingen : 1840. 8vo. pp. 8.

WALTHER (Samuel). Die Ehre der vor dreyhundert Jahren erfundenen Buchdruckerkunst, und was die Stadt Magdeburg von derselben vor Dienste und Vortheile gehabt, sollte auf obrigkeitliche Veranstaltung, den 29. Novembr. des jetztlauffenden 1740 Jahres mit einem geringen Beytrag in dem Gymnasie der alten Stadt Magdeburg, sowol durch diesen Vorbericht, als auch öffentliche Reden zum Preise Gottes. Magdeburg : [1740]. 4to. pp. 48.

The third chapter gives a history of printing in Magdeburg, and there is a chronological list of Magdeburg printers

WAPPEN der Buchdrucker (Das). Leipzig.

This is the Printers' coat-of-arms, printed in colours, on a sheet 47 centimètres by 62 centimètres in size. There is also a smaller edition, printed in colours, and in relief.

WAPPEN der Lithographen und Steindrucker in dreizehn Farben ausgeführt von Ferd. Wüst. Wien : 1880. Large 4to.

WARNSDORFF (L. von). Ueber Druckfehler. Ein Appell an das lesende und schriftstellernde Publicum, insbesondere der Zeitungen. Berlin 1879. 8vo. pp. 48.

An essay on printers' errors, the cause of many of them and the means to avoid them being explained, in defence of the printers.

WARNSINCK (W. H.). De Uitvinding der Boekdrukkunst door Lourens Janszoon Koster te Haarlem. Anno 1423. Zinnespeel : (In Loosjes Gedenkschriften, pp. 233-274.) Haarlem : 1824.

WARRANT, A., of the Lord General Fairfax to the Marshall General of the Army, to put in execution the former Ordinances and Orders * * * concerning the regulating of Printing. London : 1649. 4to. pp. 15.

Quotes the previous Orders of Parliament against irregular printers.

WAT Coster wist, wat hij niet wist, en wat hij weten megt. Haarlem : 1856. 8vo. pp. 4.

WATERLOW & SONS. A Report of the Police Proceedings in connexion with the dispute between the firm of Messrs. Waterlow & Sons and the London Printing Machine Managers' Association. London. 1882. 8vo. pp. 26.

LONDON: 1557–1591.

WATKINS (Richard).

This printer lived in St. Paul's churchyard, and had a shop adjoining to the "Little Conduit in Cheap." He possessed a patent, in conjunction with James Roberts, for printing almanacks, and was warden of the Stationers' Company in 1583. He then gave up his rights of publishing the sheet or broadside almanack, devoting the proceeds to the relief of the poor belonging to the Company. He used, besides the above device, one in which the chief feature was a sitting hare or rabbit.

WATON (Aug.). Étude des calcaires lithographiques de la Ligurie, etc., précédée d'une notice historique sur la découverte et le progrès de l'art de la lithographie, etc. Impr. Chaix. Paris: 1878. 8vo. pp. iii., 210.

[WATSON (James)]. The History of the Art of Printing, containing an Account of It's Invention and Progress in Europe: with the Names of the Famous Printers, the Places of their Birth, and the Works printed by them. With a Preface by the Publisher to the Printers in Scotland. Printed by James Watson. Edinburgh: 1713. 8vo. Sold at his Shop opposite to the Lucken-Booths. Preface, pp. 24; Specimen of Types, pp. xlviii.; History of Printing, pp. 64.

"At best but a meagre performance; it happens to be rare, and, therefore, bibliomaniacs hunt after it." So writes Dr. Dibdin ("Bibliomania," p. 69) in his usual superficial style. He is right so far as rarity goes, for it is a volume that must be waited and watched for ; but that is not its only recommendation, for it contains some interesting and useful information on Scotch Printing not found elsewhere. The didactic part, as stated in the preface, was written by John Spottiswoode, translated from a celebrated French writer ; this was La Caille, who, in 1689, published his "Histoire de l'Imprimerie."

—— A previous View of the Case between John Baskett, Esq., one of His Majesty's Printers, plaintiff, and Henry Parsons, Stationer, defendant. Printed by James Watson, one of His Majesty's Printers. Edinburgh : [1717]. 4to. pp. 35.

Extremely well printed.

JAMES WATSON, whose "History of Printing" is above noticed, claimed, as Printer to His Majesty in Scotland, the right of printing the Bible and of selling it anywhere in the United Kingdom. Henry Parsons was his agent. There can be little doubt that Watson wrote this clever tract (which is thus dated in the catalogue of the British Museum, but Mr. Blades gives 1720 as the year of its appearance), and his argument is, that the Act of Union between England and Scotland having stipulated equality and complete freedom of trade between the two countries, Mr. Baskett, King's Printer in England, while claiming the privilege of printing Bibles and selling them in Scotland, prosecuted Mr. Parsons for selling in England Bibles printed by Mr. Watson in Scotland. Incidentally is mentioned the fact of Baskett having leased the Printing-house at Oxford for Bible-printing, as did also Thomas Guy (Guy's Hospital) for a few years.

WATT (P. B.). A few Hints on Colour and Printing in Colours. London : 1872. 8vo. pp. 32.

The author, who is a practical lithographer and has had experience abroad as well as in England, was the originator, and for some time part proprietor, of *The Lithographer*, in establishing which publication he spent much time and money. The substance of this little work appeared first in the pages of the above publication, July and August, 1870, and January, 1871. (*See Lithographer*, PERIODICAL PUBLICATIONS.)

WATT (Robert), M.D. Bibliotheca Britannica ; or, a general Index to British and Foreign Literature. In two parts, Authors and Subjects. Edinburgh : 1824. 4to. 4 vols.

"Upon the early printing, both of this country and the Continent, much pains have been bestowed. All the early British printers noticed by Ames, Herbert, and Dibdin have been inserted, and the works arranged both under the printers' names and their respective authors. Notices, equally full, and from other sources, have been given, of every early foreign printer of any eminence, and the works entered under these are, in like manner, given under their authors. There is thus condensed, into this part of the work, the substance of all that has been published with regard to the early history of printing."—*Preface.*

DR. ROBERT WATT was a physician ; born 1774. He became president of the Faculty of Physicians and Surgeons at Glasgow, and died there in 1819. His "Bibliotheca Britannica" is an invaluable work to the bibliographer, and a stupendous monument of industry. It was completed and issued by his son, who says in the preface : "The account given of British writers and their works is universal, embracing every description of authors, and every branch of knowledge and literature. What has been admitted of foreign publications, though selective, forms a very considerable and valuable portion of the work ; and as none of note have been purposely omitted, the 'Bibliotheca Britannica' may be considered as a useful catalogue of all the authors with which this country is acquainted, whether of its own or of the Continent."

See articles, *s. v.* Typography, Stationer, Stereotype, Press, Paper, Papermaker, Paper-marks, Paper-mill, Engraver, Engraving. The books under the heading "Lithography" are on geology and palæontology.

WATTS (Thomas). A Letter to Antonio Panizzi, Esq., Keeper of the Printed Books in the British Museum, on the reputed Earliest Printed Newspaper, *The English Mercurie*, 1588. London: 1839. 8vo. pp. 16.

This letter dissipates the idea which, up to 1839, was generally current that England was the first country to print a newspaper.

Mr. THOMAS WATTS was the keeper of the department of printed books, British Museum. Having discovered in his visits to the reading-room the absence of Russian and Hungarian literature from the library, and the great deficiencies in other modern languages, he published some letters and suggestions on the subject. In 1838 he obtained an appointment in the Museum, became assistant-keeper of printed books, and superintendent of the reading-room, and about 1866 was advanced to be keeper of the printed books He wrote a large number of biographical articles for encyclopædias and reviews. Died 1869.

WAUTERS (Alphonse). Documents pour servir à l'histoire de l'Imprimerie dans l'ancien Brabant. [In the *Bulletin du Bibliophile Belge*, vol. xiii. pp. 73-84. Bruxelles: 1856. 8vo.]

The author is one of the best historians of Belgium and the Netherlands. His "Table chronologique des chartes et diplômes imprimés concernant l'histoire de la Belgique" includes references to printing and publishing.

WEBER (Ferd.). Beschreibung des Gutenberg-Festes in Elberfeld am 25. Juli 1840. Elberfeld: 1840. 8vo. pp. 48.

WEBERS (J. G.). Weimarischer Beitrag zu feyerlicher Begehung des dritten 100 jährigen Jubel-Festes einer wohllöblichen Buchdruckerkunst. Darinnen nebst der dabey · gehaltenen Predigt, andre dahin gehörige Betrachtungen enthalten. Nebst einer Vorrede. Weimar 1740. 8vo. 12 leaves and pp. 136.

FRANKFORT-AM-MAIN: 1573-1581.

WECHEL (Andreas).

The device of this printer consists of Pegasus and a caduceus, between two horns of abundance, borne by two clasped hands.

WECHEL (Johan).

The annexed device of this printer represents Minerva leaning on a wand, with the caduceus and horns of abundance, surmounted by the owl : on a shield is the letter W on the prolonged down-stroke of the figure 4.

FRANKFORT-AM-MAIN : 1591.

WEDDING. Beschreibung einer von C. A. Holm in London erfundenen, von den Mechanikern Nasmyth, Caskell, & Co. in Manchester gebauten Skandinavien-Presse. Berlin : 1845. 4to. pp. 12. 3 plates.

The author was the director of the Prussian State Printing-office, and his essay was a reprint from the Transactions of the Society for Promoting Industry in Prussia.

WEDMORE (Frederick). Masters of Etching. Articles in *Macmillan's Magazine*, 1874.

———— Four Masters of Etching. With original etchings by Haden, Jacquemart, Whistler, and Legros. London : 1883. 4to. pp. 46.

W(EGELIN) (P.). Die Buchdruckereien der Schweiz. Mit erläuternden und ergänzenden Anmerkungen. Eine Gelegenheitsschrift, zur Feier des vierten Jubelfestes der Erfindung der Buchdruckerkunst. St. Gallen : 1836. 8vo. pp. xx. 180; appendix, pp. 34.

———— Geschichte der Buchdruckereien im Kanton St. Gallen. Mit einleitender Nachricht über die Erfindung der Buchdruckerkunst. Eine Festgabe für die Theilnehmer an der Säkularfeier in St. Gallen am 24. Juni 1840. St. Gallen : 1840. 8vo. pp. vii. 108.

WEILLE (J. H.). Die Zeitung. Ihre Organisation und Technik. Versuch eines journalistischen Handbuchs. Wien : 1883. 8vo. pp. viii. 309.

———— Das Buch. Technik der Schriftstellerei. Versuch eines Handbuches für Autoren. Wien : 1879. 8vo. pp. iv. 236.

In the first book, the author aims at giving an insight into the technicalities of getting out a daily paper, and in the second into the printing of a book, for the benefit of inexperienced journalists and young authors. Both books are of practical value.

WEHRHAN (Otto Fr.). Gutenbergs erster Druck, oder facsimile der ersten Seite des ersten in der Welt gedruckten Buches. Bei Gelegenheit der iv. Säcularfeier des Typendruckes mit einer kurzen geschichtlichen Erläuterung herausgegeben. Leipzig : 1840. Folio. 1 leaf.

WEIGEL (Theordor Oswald). Catalogue de Premières productions de l'art d'Imprimerie en possession de Mr. T. O. Weigel. French title of the following work :—

———— Ars Moriendi. Editio princeps. Photographisches facsimile. Leipzig : 1869. 4to.

———— Katalog frühester Erzeugnisse der Druckerkunst der Weigelschen Sammlung. Zeugdrucke, Metallschnitte, Holzschnitte, etc. Mit 12 Abbildungen. Leipzig : 1872. 8vo. pp. viii. 274. This is the most scientifically prepared catalogue ever issued.

———— Verzeichniss der xylographischen Bücher des fünfzehnten Jahrhunderts. Leipzig : 1856. 8vo. pp. 10. One hundred copies only reprinted from the *Serapeum.*

WEIGEL (T. O.) and ZESTERMANN (Ad.). Collectio Weigeliana. Die Anfänge der Druckeskunst in Bild und Schrift. An deren frühesten Erzeugnissen in der Weigel'schen Sammlung erläutert. 2 vols. with 145 facsimiles and woodcuts in the text. Leipzig : 1866. Folio. Two parts.

Of this edition 325 copies were printed. "This magnificent work is the most perfect sample of the art of Printing and facsimile engraving ever produced in Germany. The author's design is to show that the first discovery of Printing with movable characters, words, lines, and entire pages, and reproducing by means of colour, belongs to the Germans and not to the Dutch. Impressions on cotton-cloth, engravings on metal, wood, paste, and copper, are to be found in the work." The Collectio-Wergeliana contains a wonderful collection of early prints or engravings and blockbooks ; referred to by Hessels (Gutenberg), p. 7. This work, with Berjeau (Catalogue Illustre), has done much towards the compilation of a list or catalogue of all the prints and engravings or blockbooks which have been discovered, but a complete catalogue is still a desideratum.

WEIJER (P. W. van de). Proeven van Reproductie van oude Drukwerken (MS. title). Utrecht : 1864. A collection of six leaves of litho. facsimiles of works printed between 1446 and 1709.

WEIMAR. Zur Geschichte der Hof-Buchdruckerei in Weimar. Weimar : 1858. 8vo. pp. 16.

———— *See* WEBERS.

WEIMARS Album zur vierten Säcularfeier der Buchdruckerkunst am 24. Juni 1840. Weimar : 1840. Royal 8vo. pp. iv., six leaves of list of subscribers, pp. 356, six copperplates.

A collection of essays contributed by various writers. Among them are a History of the State Printing House of Weimar, by Dr. Panse ; a sermon by Dr. J. F. Rœhr, and nineteen other literary articles on Goethe, &c.

WEISE (Adam).   Albrecht Dürer und sein Zeitalter.   Leipzig : 1819. 4to.   Portrait.

WEISHAUPT (Heinrich).   Das Gesammtgebiet des Steindrucks, oder vollständige theor tisch-praktische Anweisung zur Ausübung der Lithographie in ihrem ganzen Umfange und auf ihrem jetzigen Standpunkte.   Nebst einem Anhange von der Zinkographie, dem Anastatischen Drucke und der Photolithographie.   Weimar : 1875. 16mo.   pp. xvi., 563.   With an accompanying Atlas, giving on 12 double-page plates some 140 illustrations of lithographic presses and other material.

A treatise, both theoretical and practical, on the art of Lithography. The author was one of the Professors at the Technological Institute at Munich, and a son of the F. Weishaupt mentioned by Senefelder in his work on Lithography. After a brief history of the art, come some remarks on the relative value which copperplate printing, wood engraving, and lithography bear to each other. The different processes practised in connexion with the last-mentioned art are next passed in review, and after this the author dives *in medias res*, and deals with all that belongs to lithography, chromo-lithography, zincography, and the many other intercorrelated chemical and heliographic processes. The illustrations in the Atlas, to which frequent reference is made in the text, have all been neatly executed in lithography.

—— Theoretisch-praktische Anleitung zur Chromo-Lithographie oder zum lithogr.   Farbendruck, sowie zu lithographischem Kunstdruck überhaupt.   Mit 4 lithogr. Tafeln.   Quedlinburg and Leipzig : 1848.   8vo.   pp viii. and 168.

WEISS (C. E.).—*See* RATTWITZ.

WEISS (Julius).   Die Galvanoplastik, oder sichere Anleitung und ausführliche Darstellung des galvanoplastischen Verfahrens in all' seinen Theilen.   Wien : 1878.   8vo.   pp. viii. 302.   [Editions also published at Pesth and Leipzig.]   Second edition, 1883.

The different galvanoplastic processes are very clearly explained in this handbook, diagrams helping to make the matter more easily understood.

WEISS (M.).   Specimens of the Printing Establishment of M. Weiss. Malta : 1845.   8vo.

Types of various kinds, ornaments, and 211 wood or metal cuts.

WEISSENBACH (Hanns von).   Der xylographische Farbendruck in den verschiedenen Phasen seiner Herstellung, erläutert an dem Titelbild des Missale Romanum, edit. Henricus Reiss 1861. Nürnberg : 1878.   Folio.   Twenty-four chromo-xylographies and four pages of explanations.

Shows, by examples, the progress of a chromo-xylographic picture, from the first printing to its completion.

WEISSENBURGER (Johann).

This well-known German printer established his press, first of all, at Nuremberg, in 1503.   Ten years later he removed to Landshut, where he continued to print till 1531.   The results of his typographical career, extending over twenty-eight years, are enumerated in Panzer. The device used at both places by

Weissenburger—which we reproduce— the globe are the letters H H (whose
consists of the emblem of the Globe and precise signification is not known, being,

NUREMBERG, 1503–1513; LANDSHUT, 1513–1531.

Cross. The latter is surmounted by a perhaps, that of some publisher) and W,
pennon or pendant. On either side of the initial of the printer's surname.

L

74 *Bibliography of Printing.*

WEISTRITZ (Philander von der). Lebensbeschreibung des berühmten und gelehrten Dänischen Sternschers Tycho v. Brahes. Aus den Dänischen Sprache in die Deutsche übersetzt. Kopenhagen und Leipzig : 1756. 8vo.
From the Danish of Herr Oluf Bang. Quoted by Blades, " Numismata Typographica."

WELCKER (Philipp Heinrich). Festgedicht bei der vierten Säcularfeier der Buchdruckerkunst und beim Jubiläum des zweihundertjährigen Bestehens der Engelhard-Reyherschen Buchdruckerei in Gotha, im grossen Saal derselben gesprochen von Ph. II. Welcker, den 24. Juni 1840. Gotha : 1840. 8vo. 24 pp. of poetry.

WELDAAD (De) der Boekdrukkunst voor het menschelijk geslacht, dankbaar herdacht bijde onthulling van het metalen standbeeld ter eere van Laurens Janszoon Coster, te Haarlem, den 16en July 1856. 's Gravenhage : 1857. 8vo. pp. 47.

WELLER (Emil). Repertorium typographicum. Die deutsche Literatur im ersten Viertel des sechzehnten Jahrhunderts. Im Anschluss an Hains Repertorium u. Panzers deutsche Annalen. Second title : Gg. Wolf. Panzers Annalen der älteren deutschen Literatur 1500–26. Dritter Theil. Nach den Quellen bearbeitet. Nördlingen 1864. 8vo. pp. xviii. 506.——Supplement. Nordlingen 1874. 8vo. pp. iv. 70.
There is a second title-page which reads : "G. W. Panzer's Annalen der älteren deutschen Literatur 1500-1526. Dritter Theil."

——— Die falschen und fingerten Druckorte. Repertorium der seit Erfindung der Buchdruckerkunst unter falscher Firma erschienenen deutschen, lateinischen und französischen Schriften. 2 vols. Leipzig 1864. 8vo.

WELZENBACH (Thomas). Geschichte der Buchdruckerkunst im ehemaligen Herzogthum Franken und in den benachbarten Fränkischen Städten. Würzburg : 1858. 8vo.

WENG (J. F.). Antiquissima quædam typographiæ monumenta hactenus incognita in Bibliotheca civitatis Nordlingensis asservata. Nordlingæ : 1816. 4to.

WERDET (Edmond). De la Librairie Française. Son passé, son présent, son avenir. Paris : 1860. 12mo. 3 leaves and pp. 394.
Containing a short historical account of Printing, and the biographies of several Printers.

——— Histoire du Livre en France, depuis les temps les plus reculés jusqu'en 1860. 6 vols. Paris : 1861-64. 8vo.
The fourth part only containing the History of the Press in the French Provinces ; also of private and clandestine Presses.

——— Extrait de l'Histoire du Livre en France. Études Bibliographiques sur la famille des Didot, Imprimeurs, Libraires, Graveurs, Fondeurs de Caractères, Fabricants de Papiers, etc. (1713–1864). Paris : 1864. 8vo. pp. 47.

This is an extract from the above work, and gives a detailed account of the celebrated Didot family. One hundred copies were reprinted from "L'histoire du Livre en France," of which twenty were for sale. The author describes himself on the title-page as "ancien libraire-éditeur à Champs-parchelles, Seine-et-Marne."

A new work has been announced as in preparation, entitled : "De l'imprimerie Française et des arts et industries qui s'y rapportent ; nus à la portée des gens du monde, des savants, et des gens de lettres, avec des notices bibliographiques sur les imprimeurs, les protes, les correcteurs, les ouvriers typographes et les libraires les plus célèbres et distingués de Paris depuis 1789 jusqu'à nos jours."

WERNER (Ferd.). Die Galvanoplastik in ihrer technischen Anwendung. St. Petersburg : 1844. Royal 8vo. 12 copper plates.

WERNIGERODISCHES Dank- und Jubelfest, wegen der erfundenen Buchdruckerkunst. Wernigerode. 1740. 4to.

WERTHER (Johann David). Wahrhafftige Nachrichten der so alt- als berühmten Buckdruckerkunst, in welchen vom Ursprung und Fortgang der Buchdruckereyen, von 1440 an biss jetzo 1721, und denen darin eingeführten Gebräuchen, auch eingeschlichenen Missbräuchen und Unordnungen, gehandelt wird. Alles aus bewährtesten Urkunden und selbst-eigener vieljahrigen Erfahrung mit grossem Fleiss und Kosten zusammen getragen und aus unpartheyischen Gemüthe dem Publico mitgetheilet. Franckfurth und Leipzig 1721. 4to. pp. xxiv. 504.

This work abounds with most curious information about the manner in which the printing trade was carried on in Germany during the seventeenth century. The author was a practical printer, and in the preface he expresses regret that it is more and more becoming the fashion to discard old traditions in connexion with the craft, and that the rising generation consider themselves more clever and superior to those who have had many years' experience of the trade. In the face of that revolutionary spirit which prompted the younger printers to urge new-fangled customs and regulations upon their elder brethren, the writer says he felt called upon to stem the tide of innovation. Touching upon the history of the invention of Typography, he propounds the following amusing theory:—About 1440, a Strasburg citizen named Johann Mäntelein commenced experiments in that direction, without, however, meeting with much success. He took into his service one Hanss Gänsefleischen, to whom he communicated some particulars concerning the invention. The latter abused the confidence reposed in him, and reported all he had been told to Johann Guttenbergen, a Mayence citizen of great wealth, who, after ruining himself in continuing the experiments, fell in with Johann Faust, when their united efforts brought the invention to a successful issue.

The extent to which sumptuary legislation interfered with the pursuit of the printing trade is amply illustrated by the many enactments which are here reproduced, as to the number of apprentices to be employed in different offices. The town council of Nuremberg, for example, ordained, in 1673, that no master-printer should have more *employés*, and especially apprentices, than was found absolutely necessary. Only one boy was to be allowed above the number engaged at press or case, for taking proofs out, and for doing other extraneous labour. He was not, however, allowed to be apprenticed until one of the others had completed his time. At Hamburg the civic authorities went, however, much further ; they enjoined that no journeyman-printer should marry any other woman than one of unexceptionable morals, and who was able to adduce a certificate of legitimate birth and of good behaviour. In many parts of Germany it was enjoined that no contract between master and journeyman was to be other than a half-yearly one. Any employer sheltering a journeyman who had illegally absented himself from work was to be held guilty as a criminal. The establishment of a sick fund in each printing-office was also made obligatory by more than one town council, even the amount being fixed which masters and journeymen were severally to pay. A proviso was, however, added, that no printer who was in the habit of carousing or rioting was to enjoy any benefit from the fund. The German journeymen of the seventeenth century would seem to have been somewhat addicted to high living, for it is specially laid down by the Nuremberg authorities that "all feasting, tippling, and gaming" in printing-offices is to be discontinued. Exception is also taken to the carousing indulged in on the occasion of an apprentice attaining to journeyman's estate, "which has often cost twenty thalers (£3) and more, and which has brought many a journeyman to poverty and induced him to run into debt." No more than £1. 16s. or at most £2. 8s. is, after the date of this enactment (February, 1673), to be spent on such an occasion; "no females to be admitted to the feast."

Many incidents are related in this book demonstrative of the spirit of exclusiveness which obtained two centuries ago in the printing, as in other guilds. No one who had not been duly apprenticed to the trade was allowed to carry on business on his own account. In Constanz (on the borders of Switzerland), for example, the son of one David Haut inherited the printing-office of his father after the latter's death. The two journeymen in his employ afterwards discovered that their master had never been apprenticed to the art of Printing, but to that of type-founding. They consequently struck work, in which course of action they were joined by the apprentices. Haut called in the aid of the Lucerne authorities, but the men escaped into the "Holy Roman Empire," where they had the support of the German printing guilds, which latter held the conduct of the men to have been "faithful and true." It is amusing to read that, "although Haut was left in possession of his printing-office, it was ordained that no youth apprenticed to him should be considered to have properly learned his trade." In Stockholm, a master-bookbinder named Keiser, advanced in

years, similarly inherited a printing-office. He, in consequence, proceeded to Hamburg, requesting the local guild to allow him to be apprenticed to the craft. His wish was complied with, and a manager was appointed, to whom he was apprenticed, and who, meanwhile, took the superintendence of the Stockholm establishment. Having completed his term of service he was declared free of the Hamburg guild. The question of apprenticeship continued a fruitful source of discord. Again and again regulations were passed to limit the number of boys in printing-offices, and those who had served with masters who employed boy labour, either exclusively or to a disproportionate extent, were not admitted to the ranks of the journeymen. Despite all enactments, however, boy labour continued to flourish, although the proprietors of such so-called "hedge presses" were held in great contempt both by masters and men.

From an edict issued by the Dantzig Town Council, and given, *in extenso*, by Werther, it would appear that the employers as well as the employed had a right to a certain number of copies of any work printed in their establishment. It is provided, by an enactment of the year 1660, that the author shall have the right to redeem the copies in question, while in no case was it legal to dispose of these presentation copies before the complete work had been delivered to the author. Printers were also threatened with imprisonment and the recovery of damages if they struck off any extra copies besides those ordered by the author. Many other and no less interesting particulars are given in the above work, which contains, in addition, the names of successive early printers in many German towns, and the seals of several printing corporations are also figured.

The above synopsis conveys a fair idea of the curious contents of the volume, and the reading-matter of the title-page being no less quaint, it may be of interest to append an English translation thereof: —"True Intelligence of the no-less-old than famous art of Typography, in which is treated of the origin and progress of printing-offices from 1440 up to the present 1721, and of the customs which now obtain therein, and of the abuses and irregularities which have crept in. All compiled with great diligence and at great cost, from the most reliable sources and from individual experience of many years, and communicated in an impartial spirit to the public by Johann David

Werther, Franckfurth and Leipzig.
To be found by Johann Felix Bieleken."
A criticism of this volume was after-
wards published under the title : "Der
Jenaischen Buchdrucker - Gesellschaft
nöthige Anmerkungen und erlaubte
Zugaben, so da zeigen wie partheyisch,

unkunstmässig und straffbahr Johann
David Werther zu Jena, bey Edirung
der sogenannten wahrhafftigen Nachrichten von der berühmten Buchdruckerkunst, sich aufgeführet." (Jena : 1721.
4to. pp. viii. 104.) The preface is signed
by the Printers' Society of Jena.

WESSELY (J. E.). Anleitung zur Kenntniss und zum Sammeln der
Werke des Kunstdruckes. Mit zwei Tafeln Monogramme.
- Leipzig : 1876 8vo. pp. viii. 338.

Treats on wood-engraving, copperplate-engraving, lithography, paper and paper-
marks ; gives information about the quality and value of prints, rules for making
collections, &c., and is altogether a very useful book.

——— Zur Geschichte des Farbendruckes. (In Westermann's
Illustr. Monatshefte April, 1880, No. 283, Braunschweig.)
pp. 11, with illustrations.

W[EST] (W.). Fifty Years' Recollections of an Old Bookseller ;
consisting of Anecdotes, Characteristic Sketches, and Original
Traits and Eccentricities of Authors, Artists, Actors, Books,
Booksellers, and of the Periodical Press for the last Half Century,
with appropriate selections ; and an unlimited Retrospect, including some extraordinary circumstances relative to the Letters
of Junius, and a chain of corroborative evidence respecting their
Author. Cork : 1835. 8vo.

——— Three hundred and fifty Years' Retrospection of an Old Bookseller ; containing an account of the Origin and Progress of Printing,
Type Founding, and Engraving, in their various branches ; also
the Origin of the earliest Books, Pamphlets, Magazines, Reviews,
Periodical Essays and Newspapers ; with Biographical Anecdotes
and Portraits. Cork : 1835. 8vo. pp. 200.

It is curious to see a bookseller adopt
the absurd plan of noting the contents
of the second half of his book by a fresh
title. Here we have title-page as above
and prospectus, or two leaves, inserted
between pp. 100 and 101. There are
eight plates, including portraits of the

Author, his "Literary Laboratory," the
Politician, Chris. Brown, Francis Grose,
John Dunton, John Nichols, Edward
Cave, and William Bowyer. It is an
extremely curious and amusing work,
and deserves more attention than it has
received.

WESTEN (Petersen). Historisk efterreding om Bogtrykkerkonsten.
Odense : 1873. 8vo. pp. iv. 50.

WESTERMANN's Holzschnitt-Illustrations-Katalog. Zum Gebrauche
für Buchhändler und Buchdrucker. Enthaltend 2,557 Num-
mern. Braunschweig : 1865. 4to. pp. xvi. 336.

——— Erster Nachtrag. Enthaltend No. 2558-2854. Braunschweig : 1866. 4to. pp. 337-396. 4 leaves.

——— Zweiter Nachtrag. Enthaltend No. 2855-3174. Braunschweig : 1867. 4to. pp. 397-444. 3 leaves.

—— Dritter Nachtrag.   Enthaltend No. 3175–3424.   Braunschweig : 1870.   4to.   pp. 445 504.   4 leaves.

—— · Vierter Nachtrag.   Enthaltend No. 3425–4115.   Braunschweig : 1874.   4to.   pp. 505-636.   6 leaves.

—— Fünfter Nachtrag.   Enthaltend No. 4116–4592.   Braun schweig : 1879.   4to.   pp. 637–728.   4 leaves.

—— Sechster Nachtrag.   Enthaltend No. 4593–5063.   Braunschweig : 1882.   4to.   pp. 729-824.   5 leaves.

WESTERMANN (G.).   Namen und Sachregister von Westermann's Holzschnitt - Illustrations - Katalog.   Nachweisung über die' in demselben abgedruckten 3174 Holzschnitte.   Braunschweig : 1868.   8vo.   pp. 40.

WESTFEHLING (J.).   Gutenberg.   Eine Biographie, zusammengestellt und nach verschiedenen Quellen bearbeitet.   Winterthur : 1878.   4to.   pp. 8.   Not for sale.

This biographical sketch was drawn up by J. Westfehling, a master-printer at Winterthur, in Switzerland, and dedicated by him to his employés on the occasion of the completion of the 25th year of his trade-membership.   It has been very elegantly printed.

WESTREENEN van TIELLANDT (W. H. J. Baron van).   1. Iets over de afbeeldingen van Laurens Jansz. Koster door Baron van Westreenen van Tiellandt.   's Gravenhage : 1847.   8vo. and 12mo.   pp. 16.
Reprinted from the " Journal de Tyd."

—— 2. Bewijzen voor de echtheid en gelijkenis der oude afbeeldingen van Koster : Haarlem : 1847.   4to. and 8vo.

—— 3. De zoogenaamde " Bewijzen voor de echtheid en gelijkenis der oude afbeeldingen van Koster," wederlegd door den Baron van Westreenen van Tiellandt.   's Gravenhage : 1848. 8vo.   pp. 10.

—— Jets over Stereotypen.   Haarlem : 1801.   8vo.   Reprinted from the "Algemeene Konst. en Letterbode" von 16 October, 1801.   No. 42.

—— Korte schets van den voortgang der Boekdrukkunst in Nederland, in de xve en haare verdere volmaaking in de 16e en 17e eeuw.   's Gravenhage en Amsterdam : 1829.   8vo.   pp. 37.
Entirely superseded by later researches.

—— Nasporingen nopens de invoering der boekdrukkunst. 's Gravenhage : 1828.   In the " Konst. en Letterbode," No. 53, 1828.

—— Rapport sur les recherches relatives à l'invention de l'Imprimerie Stéréotype.   La Haye : 1866.   8vo.   With plates.

—— Verslag der Naspooringen omtrent de oorsprongkelijke uitvinding en het vroegste Gebruik der Stereotypische Drukwijze : —gedaan, op uitnoodiging van het Gouvernement. 's Gravenhage : 1833. 8vo. pp. 61 and 4 plates, in French and Dutch.

The author claims the priority of the invention of Stereotype for the Rev. Jean Muller, pastor, of Leyden, whose son, William Muller, printed from plates of types soldered together in movable pages, several Bibles and Testaments in Syriac, Dutch, and English, between 1708 and 1716. In 1716, Van der Mey took casts of pages in plaster of Paris, and made plates.

—— Verhandeling over de Uitvinding der Boekdrukkunst ; in Holland oorspronkelijk uitgedacht, te Straatsburg verbeterd en te Mentz voltooid. 's Hage : 1809. 8vo. pp. 184.

WETSTEIN (H. F.). Letterproef van de Gieterij van Hendrik Floris Wetstein tot Amsterdam. [n.d.]

A demy sheet, in the Enschedé collection. The founts are shown in four columns. There are two titling founts, six Greek (text to collonel), fifteen Roman, fifteen Italic (both from text to diamond), four blacks, two music, one Arabic, and three others. There is nothing to show the date of publication, but it has been ascertained that H. F. Wetstein succeeded to this foundry in 1743.

WETSTEIN (R). Versameling van een Party curieuse Letteren in allerlei Soorten. Alle bij een Vergaderd, en nagelaten op de Drukkery van Wylen de Heer Rudolph Wetstein. Amsterdam : 1743. 4to.

Isaac and John Enschedé purchased the whole of this Printing-office and Foundry, which formed the foundation of the celebrated Haarlem Foundry.

WETSTEIN (R. & H. F.). Anno 1740. Épreuve des caractères de la Nouvelle Fonderie de R. & H. F. Wetstein à Amsterdam, et que l'on trouve à vendre chez eux. No. 1.

A half-sheet of Royal, in the Enschedé collection. The types are displayed in double column, and include all the sizes of Roman and Italic from "Augustyn" to "Diamant," with a Brevier Greek. The founts are beautifully cut, especially the Diamond, which has small caps, accents, signs, &c. As the names differ somewhat from those subsequently adopted they are copied here :—

Augustyn	Brevier
Mediaan	Collonel
Dessendiaan	Nomparel
Garmond	Robyn
Galijart } both same	Diamant
Grote Brevier } body	

WETTEN en verordeningen nopens den boekhandel en de drukpers in Nederland. 's Gravenhage : 1834. 8vo.

WETTER (Johann). Beantwortung der Frage : In welchem Jahre ist die Buchdruckerkunst erfunden worden, und wann ist das Säcular-fest der Erfindung zu feiern? Mainz : 1837. 8vo. pp. 48.

An argument to the effect that typography was invented by John Gutenberg at Strasbourg, about the year 1450, and that the proper date for the quarcentenary celebration should be 1850. It was held, however, in 1840.

—— Conrad Henlif oder Henekis, Buchdrucker und Buchhändler zu Mainz, der Geschäftsgenosse Peter Schoeffer's. Mainz : 1851. 8vo. pp. 15.

An unimportant little tract, wretchedly printed, in a blue tissue paper-wrapper.

———— Kritische Geschichte **der** Erfindung der Buchdruckerkunst
durch Johann Gutenberg **zu** Mainz, begleitet mit einer, vorhin
noch nie angestellten, genauen Prüfung und gänzlichen Beseitigung
der von Schöpflin und seinen Anhängern verfochtenen Ansprüche
der Stadt Strassburg, und einer **neuen** Untersuchung der
Ansprüche **der** Stadt Harlem, und vollständigen Widerlegung
ihrer Verfechter Junius, Meerman, Koning, Dibdin, Ottley, und
Ebert. Mainz : 1836. 8vo. **pp. xvi. 806.** Atlas of **13** plates of
facsimiles in folio.

A valuable work, in which many of
the documents relating to the invention
of printing are reproduced in the
original text. The plates [Tafeln] to
this work are valuable, and it may
be useful to state some of their contents for the benefit of those who are
interested in comparative typography.
The facsimiles include :—Inscription on
the St. Christopher image of 1423, belonging to Earl Spencer ; the Calendar
of John de Gamundia, of 1439 ; Image
of Indulgence, belonging to Weigel, of
Leipsic ; Ars Moriendi ; Donatus in
the King's Library, Paris ; Copy printed
from a column composed of movable
wooden types, threaded by lines, being
an imitation of the supposed first essays
of Gutenberg ; Copy printed from types
cast in leaden matrices ; copy printed
from type cast in matrices of copper ;
Donatus of 1451 ; written Psalter of

1498 ; Specimen by Pfister ; the Indul-
gences ; Calendar, 1457 ; 36-line Bible ;
Biblia Pauperum ; Fust and Schœffer's
Psalter ; 42-line Bible ; and Specimens
by the Brothers of Common Life, 1474,
W. Caxton, T. Martens, Therhoernen,
T. Rood, Valdener, Ketelare & Leempt,
G. Leeu, Sweinheim & Pannartz,
Gering, Crantz & Fribirger, Colard
Mansion, Nicolas Jenson, and J. de
Spira. These are all facsimiled in
Lithography. The titles and notes are
in German, French, and English.
Many important references to this work
will be found in Hessels's "Gutenberg :
was he the Inventor of Printing?" and
the documents reprinted, as well as the
conclusions of the former, should be
revised by the latter work, if it is desired
to arrive at the facts concerning the
origin of the art.

WHEATLEY (Henry Benjamin), F.S.A. The History and Art of
Bookbinding. An interesting lecture, with illustrations, printed
in the *Journal of the Society of Arts*, April 16, 1880.

Subsequently reprinted, with the title :—

———— Bookbinding considered as a Fine Art, Mechanical Art,
and Manufacture. A Paper read before the Society of Arts,
on Wednesday, April 14, 1880, George Bullen, Esq., F.S.A., in
the chair, and reprinted from the Journal of the Society. By
Henry B. Wheatley, F.S.A. 1882. 8vo. pp. iv. 28. 11 plates.

Although slight in parts, this compilation is worthy of notice. The engravings of ancient and famous book-
bindings are valuable. The list of the
temporary exhibition of bindings, got up
for the occasion, is also well worthy of
preservation. In the course of the dis-

cussion which followed the reading of
Mr. Wheatley's paper, Mr. George
Bullen, Mr. Cornelius Walford, Mr.
Henry Bradshaw, Mr. B. Quaritch, and
others spoke, and their views on a
subject in regard to which each is a
master, are very curious and amusing.

WHITE (Elihu). A Specimen of Printing Types from the Foundry
of E. White, New York. New York : 1817. 8vo.

A copy is in the Library of the
Antiquarian Society, Worcester, Mass.
"White was one of the earliest type-
founders in the United States. He

began to found at New York in 1810, and
soon after established foundries both at
Cincinnati and Buffalo. The business
being very successful, partners were

taken, and in 1833 a beautiful specimen book was issued under the firm of White, Hagar, & Co. Elihu White died 1839, and was succeeded by his son, John T. White, and Hagar retired. Afterwards by Charles T. White & Co. The business is now carried on under the name of Farmer, Little, & Co."—BLADES ("Type Specimen Books").

ELIHU WHITE was born at Bolton, Connecticut, of old English stock, in 1773. He began life in Hartford in the same State, and afterwards removed to New York. He was a man of great ingenuity, and made many valuable improvements in typefounding. He was also for several years a bookseller and publisher. He died at the age of sixty-three, on the 7th November, 1836,—not 1839, as stated by Mr. Blades.

WHITE (J. T.). Specimen-book of Types. New York : 1854. 4to.

WHITLOCK (J.). The Teares of the Presse ; with Reflections on the Present State of England. London : 1681. 4to.

Nine pages on the enormities of an unlicensed Press, said to have been written by J. Whitlock.

WHITTINGHAM (Charles). The Chiswick Press. Articles in the *Athenæum*, August and September, 1876.

In these articles it was stated that the executors and family of the late Mr. Whittingham had submitted their old records, correspondence, &c., to the inspection of a competent editor, with the view of compiling a History of the Chiswick Press, from about 1792 to 1860. This work has not yet appeared, and we have to refer to the above articles for anything like an adequate notice of this celebrated family—the omission of which in this BIBLIOGRAPHY would be inexcusable.

The first CHARLES WHITTINGHAM was born near Coventry, June 16, 1767, and was apprenticed to a printer. At the age of twenty-five he came to London, where he carried on the business of a printer till 1799, when he removed to Dean-street, Fetter-lane. In 1807, he removed to more commodious premises at 103, Goswell-street, where, in 1811, he took Rowland into partnership, styling the firm " Whittingham & Rowland, Printers," which continued until 1816. In 1825 the Goswell-street establishment was vacated. Meanwhile, Whittingham removed to Chiswick and set up his first press there under the management of Rowland. He was first in a house on the Mall, and then removed to College-house. The business at Chiswick was wholly his own, and carried on in his sole name till his death in January, 1840. The works printed by C. Whittingham arranged chronologically and according to the names of the several publishers, his customers, would afford an instructive lesson in London printing and publishing. This was the period of the " Legitimates" and " Pirates." The former stuck to ponderous trade editions of collected works, vaunting the costly quarto and discouraging the cheap duodecimo or handy volume. The latter in the early part of this century brought out beautiful little illustrated cheap editions of single standard poems, which had great popularity. Mr. Whittingham was offered by the Legitimate party abundant and constant work for his presses, provided he would drop the Pirates, but declined. He early turned his attention to the printing of woodcuts, and was the first who adopted the now common method of overlays in making-ready.

CHARLES WHITTINGHAM, the nephew, was born at Mitcham in Surrey, October 30, 1795 ; was apprenticed to his uncle on his removing to Chiswick, at the Stationers' Company about 1811, became a liveryman of the company in 1818, and was, for some years, a member of the Court of Assistants. His name was associated with that of his uncle, under the style of C. & C. Whittingham, from 1824 to 1830, but in August, 1828, he succeeded to the old premises of Valpy, in Tooke's-court, Chancery-lane, and set up business for himself. During his first year here, he began printing for William Pickering, the Piccadilly publisher, whose beautiful books have rendered his name famous the world over. In 1840 the nephew succeeded to the plant, goodwill, &c., of the Chiswick Press, and from that time till 1848, carried on both establishments simultaneously. In 1849 he left Tooke's-court for three years, going to Chiswick ; but in 1852 he came back to the old premises, removing his plant from Chiswick. The business is now carried on as

"Chiswick Press, Charles Whittingham & Co., Tooke's-court, Chancery-lane." In 1860, Mr. Whittingham had taken into partnership his manager, Mr. John Wilkins; he died in 1869, when the Chiswick Press reverted to Mr. Whittingham, and was conducted by Mr. J. C. Wilkins, jun., till 1871. In 1872 a triple partnership was formed by Mr. Whittingham with his sons, Charles, John, and John Charles Whittingham, and his son-in-law, Mr. B. F. Stevens, the extensive American bookseller, 4, Charing-cross. This arrangement was dissolved in 1876, Mr. Whittingham having died on the 21st of April. The business is being carried on by the executors and family, and some of its books are worthy of the reputation of its founder.

Quite recently, Mr. Henry Stevens (of Vermont), brother of Mr. B. F. Stevens, already mentioned, has issued, in a daintily-printed little book, his paper read before the Cambridge Meeting of the Library Association. It is dedicated "To the memory of two old friends, Charles Whittingham and William Pickering, printer and publisher, whose beautiful books **are** their epitaphs, and whose epitaphs **embalm** their memories." (London: 1884. 16mo.). It contains several interesting references **to the** Whittinghams.

WHO WAS CAXTON? William Caxton, Merchant, Ambassador, Historian, Author, Translator, and Printer. A Monograph. London: 1877. 8vo. Frontispiece. pp. 47.

Published anonymously, this work was really written by Mr. R. H. Blades, brother of Mr. William Blades, *the* biographer of Caxton. It was issued apropos of the celebration of 1877. It is chiefly founded on the Life by the writer's brother, and gives a good synopsis of that work in a simple and lucid style. It will be remembered that one of the most important features of Mr. William Blades's original Life and Typography was the connexion which he showed was undeniable between Caxton and Mansion of Bruges, and the very great doubt thrown upon the previously-accepted theory that the English mercer learned the art from Ulric Zell, of Cologne. Singularly enough, Mr. R. H. Blades reverts to the original theory, and says, "With all respect and deference to the judgment of so distinguished an authority, we venture to submit that it requires only a slight examination and comparison of the two types to show that," etc. The illustrations are the Red pole—Caxton's sign; and a "Printer's House of the Fifteenth Century," from Holtrop's "Monumens."

WHO WAS THE FIRST PRINTER? An article in *St. Paul's Magazine.* London: 1868. 8vo. pp. 706-718.

Records the sale just previously of the Enschedé Library at Haarlem, which was collected for the special purpose of establishing the validity of the Dutch claims, and the spirited renewal of the old dispute. The theory of the present writer is ingenious. He believes that block-printing was first carried out with success by the Dutch, some of whose enterprising traders may have learned the art from the Chinese: that a desire to economise the vast labour expended upon these page-blocks would naturally arise; that an attempt was made to turn them to further account after a sufficient number of impressions had been taken, by cutting them up into separate words or even letters; that the next step was the production of separate metal types; that the perception of the adaptability of casting to the purpose required, led directly to the adoption of movable metal types. The writer then proceeds to uphold the Koster Legend from the well-known evidence referred to, *sub voce* KOSTER.

WHYBREW (Samuel). The Progressive Printer. A book of instruction for journeymen and apprenticed printers. **Second** edition. Rochester (N.Y.): 1882. 8vo. pp. 78, 2 plates.

A very useful little work, written from a different standpoint to that of most typographical authors. The directions are very practical, and those concerning fancy composition and colour-printing especially useful. The author is partner in the firm of Whybrew & Ripley, printers and publishers, Rochester, New York.

WIAERDA (II.) Naauwkeurige verhandelinge van de eerste vinders en uytvindingen der konsten en wetenschappen. Amsterdam : 1733. 8vo.

A treatise on the discoveries and first inventors of the fine arts, including notices of the discovery of the typographic art by Coster.

WICHTIGSTE (Das) der Buchdruckerkunst für Buchhändler, Literaten und Correctoren. Leipzig : 1838. Folio. 2 leaves of tables.

WIEBEKING (C. F.) Ueber Topographische Carten. Mülheim : 1792. 4to.

WIE eine grosse Zeitung hergestellt wird. Mit Ansicht des Pavillons der *Neuen Freien Presse* auf der Wiener Weltausstellung. (In the *Gartenlaube*, No. 13, Leipzig, 1873.)

WIECHMANN-KADOW (C.M.). Beiträge zur älteren Buchdrucker-geschichte Mecklenburgs, nebst einer Zusammenstellung der bisher beschriebenen mecklenburgischen Druckdenkmale. Schwerin : 1857. 8vo. pp. 38.
Reprinted from the "Jahrb. d. Vereins f. meklenb. Geschichte," Jahrg. xxii., pp. 225-262, 1857.

——— Die meklenburgischen Formschneider des xvi. Jahrhunderts. Schwerin : 1858. 8vo. pp. 26.
Reprinted from the "Jahrb. d. Vereins f. meklenb. Geschichte," Jahrg. xxiii., pp. 101-124, 1858.

WIEDEMANN (Th.). Die kirchliche Büchercensur in der Erzdiöcese Wien. Wien : 1873. 8vo. pp. 306.

WIELAND (C.). Die Familie Schweighauser. Beitrag zur Geschichte der Typographie von Basel. Basel : 1883.
In the "Basler Jahrbuch," herausg. von A. Burckhard u. Wackernagel. Basel : 1883.

WIENER AUTOREN, die, contra den Edlen von Schönfeld, Buch-drucker und Buchhändler am Kärntnerthor. Wien : 1785. 8vo.

WIENBRAG (Ludolf). Holland in den Jahren 1831 und 1832. 2 Bände. Hamburg : 1853.
In vol. i. of "Der Harlemer Koster," pp. 190-232.

WIESENER. Mémoires sur un nouveau procédé de gravure, par Wiesener, graveur et imprimeur typographe, deposés au secré-tariat de l'Académie des Sciences le 20 Août, 1849, et le 12 Mars, 1852. Paris : 1855. 4to. pp. 8.

WIESNER (A.). Denkwürdigkeiten der österreichischen Zensur. Stuttgart : 1847. 8vo.

WIGAND. Ausführliche Beschreibung der vierten Säcularfeier der Erfindung der Buchdruckerkunst, wie sie am 24, 25, und 26. Juni 1840 zu Leipzig festlich begangen wurde, nebst einer historischen Einleitung. Leipzig : 1840. 8vo.

WIGAND'S VERLAG (Georg).   Clichés-Catalog.   Leipzig : 1869.
Folio.   78 leaves.   Vignettes 1313.

——— 1ᵉʳ Nachtrag.   Leipzig : 1876.   Folio.   36 leaves.   Vignettes
No. 1314-1900.

——— 2ᵉʳ Nachtrag.   Leipzig : 1879.   Folio.   18 leaves.   Vignettes
No. 1901-2188.

WIGHTMAN (W.).   The Amateur Printer's Handbook.   Containing
instructions for Making Printing-Presses and How to Work them
to advantage ; with practical observations and illustrations, a great
many of which are working on this principle and giving every
satisfaction.   Leeds : 1871.   8vo.

Merely an advertisement of a so-called "press," consisting of a board with a
hinged leaf, the pressure being by a handle and a cam.

WIKSSTROM (B. A.).   The True Story about Gutenberg's Invention
of Printing.   New York : 1883.   Folio.   8 leaves.

A metrical joke, illustrated in seven at the sheet he gazed, and stared and
tableaux.   1, Frederick loves Bertha ; muttered like a man demented ; the
2, and cuts her name in a bench ; 3, letters printed there might truly make
drops colour in ; 4, sitting down there- him stare, for thus the art of Printing
upon, his "teacher" Gutenberg passes ; was invented !" 7, the boy is carried off,
5, and sends him flying on to a sheet of and his "form" is used for each im-
paper ; 6, "the old man stood amazed, as pression.

WILDENHAYN (Heinr. Aug.).   Erneuerte Ehren-Gedichte auf die
Edle freye Kunst-Buchdruckerei, mit deren Ursprung, Fortgang
und Nutzbarkeit, wessen sich deren Anverwandten für andere
Künsten mit Grund der Wahrheit zu rühmen haben, mit
poetischer Feder entworfen.   Leipzig : 1743.

In Gessner's "Buchdruckerkunst."

WILKINS (Charles), Ph.D. F.R.S.   A Grammar of the Sanskrita
Language.   London : 1808.   4to.

In the preface to this work Dr. Wilkins gives an interesting account of his own
punch cutting and type-founding for the Sanskrit Grammar.

WILL & SCHUMACHER.   Holztypen-Fabrik in Mannheim Schrift-
muster.   1877.   Folio.   145 Blätter.

WILLEMS (Alphonse).   Les Elsevier : Histoire et Annales Typographiques.   Bruxelles, Paris, et La Haye : 1880.   8vo.   pp.
cclix. 607.   Plates.

This is, without doubt, one of the from the various presses of this great
best guides for those making collections house.   The above is the work referred
of Elzevir editions.   It describes with to in the BIBLIOGRAPHY, *s.v.* Elzevir,
great minuteness the principal editions *ante,* as being in preparation.

——— La première édition des Maximes de La Rochefoucauld
imprimée par les Elzevier en 1664.   Notice bibliographique.
Bruxelles : 1879.   8vo.   pp. 16.

WILLEMS (Jan Frans).   Bericht vegens de Antwerpsche Boekprinters. (pp. 69-86 of the "Mengelingen van Vaderlandschen.")

———— Berigten wegens de Boekprinters van Antwerpen, ten jare 1442, enz. door J. F. W. (Beoordeeling van -het vorenstaende berigt. [By J. Koning]. Gent : 1844. 8vo. With facsimile. pp. 61.

———— Bijdrage tot de Geschiedenis der Boekdrukkunst in Antwerpen. Antwerpen: 1828. 8vo. pp. 61, and plate.

JAN FRANS WILLEMS, the Dutch poet and scholar, was born in 1793. He attracted public attention, in 1818, by a poetical address to his countrymen, on the importance of using the tongue their fathers spoke, and in the following year appeared his "Dissertation on the Dutch Language and Literature, in con-nexion with the Southern Provinces of the Netherlands." Willems was editor of the "Belgisch Museum," of which ten volumes were published. Among his other works are a Flemish version of "Reynard the Fox," and "Miscellanies on National Subjects." He died at Ghent, in 1846.

WILLETT (Ralph). A Memoir on the Origin of Printing. Newcastle: 1817. 8vo.

42 copies printed.

———— Observations on the Origin of Printing. Newcastle : 1819. 8vo.

32 copies printed.

The Memoir on the Origin of Printing from the "Archæologia," vol. xi., pp. 267-316, edited by J. T. Brockett, was, in 1818, reprinted by the Newcastle-on-Tyne Typographical Society (*see* BROCKETT). A second edition was published in 1820, edited by Mr. T. Hodgson (*see* HODGSON). The *Harleian Miscellany* says that "this memoir has satisfactorily established the claim of Mentz to the honour of the invention." The Observations on the Origin of Printing, in a Letter to O. S. Brereton, by Ralph Willet, were also first printed in the Archæologia, vol. viii., pp. 239-250, and the reprint was edited by Mr. John Murray. Thirty-two copies only were printed, at the instance of the Newcastle-on-Tyne Typographical Society.

———— Memoir on the Origin of Printing. Addressed to John Topham, Esq., F.R. and A.SS. 50 pages from vol. xi. of "Archeologia," published separately (1793).

WILLICH (C. G.). Annalium typographicorum specimen, sive catalogus editionum ab annum 1466-1500 in Bibliotheca Annæbergensi exstantium [In his "Arcana Bibliotheca Annæbergensia. Leipzig : 1730. 8vo. pp. 298-332].

WILLSHIRE (William Hughes), M.D. An introduction to the Study and Collection of Ancient Prints. Illustrated with frontispiece, two large folding plates, being facsimiles of two unique En-gravings in the *Manière criblée*, and Monograms of Artists, 1873. Second edition, revised and enlarged, with the Marks of celebrated Collectors found on rare Prints. 2 vols. Royal 8vo. London 1874. pp. xii, 569.

A standard work on the subject. The contents include engraving in ancient times ; progress of the art from the thirteenth to the fifteenth century ; processes of engraving ; advice on com-mencing the study and collection of prints ; the various schools of engraving —the Northern and the Southern ; on chiaroscuro, metal-engraving, etching, the dotted manner, mezzotinto, examina-tion and purchase of ancient prints ; conservation and arrangement of prints. There is also a very valuable lliblio-graphy, and a table of monograms and ciphers used by engravers.

———— A Descriptive Catalogue of Playing and other Cards in the British Museum, accompanied by a concise general history of the subject and **remarks on cards** of divination, and of a politico-historical character. [London] : Printed by order of the Trustees, 1876. 8vo.

———— Supplement, with illustrations. London : 1877. 8vo. pp. xii. 87.

The plates, twenty-three in number, are printed in. colours, and form exact facsimiles of the original cards.

———— A Descriptive Catalogue of **Early Prints in the British Museum.** Vol. I., German and **Flemish Schools.** London : 1880. 8vo. pp. xii. 347. 10 plates.

WILLSON (James Renwick). Alphabetical Printing and Writing. London : 1826.

WILME (B. P.). A Manual of Writing and Printing Characters, both ancient and modern, for the use of architects, engineers, and surveyors, engravers, printers, decorators, and draughtsmen ; also for use in schools and private families, in which the various alphabets in every-day use are completely analysed and familiarly explained ; containing numerous examples of curious ancient alphabets. Illustrated with twenty-six large plates and seventeen woodcuts. London : Published for the author, 1845. 4to.

WILSON (Dr. Alexander). A Specimen of some of the Printing Types cast in the Foundery of Dr. A. Wilson & Sons, College of Glasgow. [Glasgow] : 1772. 8vo. 24 leaves.

The only types shown are Roman and Italic.

———— A Specimen of Printing-Types. At foot is :—" The above are some of the sizes cast in the Letter-Foundery of Dr. Alexander Wilson & Sons." Glasgow : 1783. Large post broadside, printed one side.

———— A Specimen of Printing-Types cast in the Letter Foundry of Alexander Wilson & Sons. Glasgow : 1786. 8vo.

———— A Specimen of Printing-Types cast in the Letter Foundry of Alexander Wilson & Sons. Glasgow : 1789. 8vo.

There is an annotation in this BIBLIOGRAPHY, *s. v.* BAINE, which is liable to misapprehension. The "Specimen of Printing Types by John Baine" (Edinburgh, 1787, 8vo.), emanated from a foundry that had a common origin with that of Dr. Wilson's, of which the specimen books are enumerated above. John Baine, the Edinburgh typefounder, sent over to Philadelphia at the close of the Revolutionary War, under the charge of a relative, probably his grandson, a complete type-foundry. About 1777 he followed himself. This was the first regular type-foundry in the United States. Baine died in 1790, and his grandson returned to England.

Struck with the idea of improving the art of printing by a new stereotyping process, Dr. Alexander Wilson and the elder Baine mentioned above joined partnership in a type-foundry which was started in St. Andrew's, Scotland, in 1742, being the first in that country. In 1744 they removed to Glasgow. In 1747 Baine went to Dublin to establish there a branch business. In 1749 the partnership was dissolved. Dr. Wilson remained in Glasgow, and there those beautiful types were produced which have gained a European renown for the press of the Foulis Brothers. Baine came back to Scotland and settled at Edinburgh ; thence he went to America, as above stated, and died there. On the death of Dr. Wilson, his foundry was carried on by his two sons, and in 1830 descended to his grandson, Alexander Wilson. In 1850 it was incorporated with the Caslon Foundry. Mr. Wilson returned to London, where he died, November 7th, 1874.

WILSON (A. J.). The Walter Press [article in *Macmillan's Magazine*, London, February, 1875, 8vo.].

Reprinted in "The Walter Press" (London : 1876, 16mo.).—*See* WALTER (J.), *ante.*

WILSON (Andrew). Arbitration between the University of Cambridge and Andrew Wilson. London : 1806. 8vo.

ANDREW WILSON was a London printer, associated with Earl Stanhope in perfecting the plaster process of stereotyping. He issued a prospectus announcing the results achieved, and in 1803, under his lordship's patronage, commenced business as a stereotyper, in which he continued for several years. He did not receive much encouragement and then took to publishing, without success. In 1804 the invention was offered to the University of Cambridge, but differences arose, and the matter fell to the ground. Wilson's account of the transaction is contained in the above pamphlet. Some misunderstanding then occurred between the patron and the printer, and Walker, who constructed the Stanhope Press and fitted up Wilson's foundry, set up in opposition to him as a stereotyper. A mechanic named Kier was then employed by Wilson to make the apparatus. Walker afterwards, to revenge himself on Wilson, announced that he would, for £30, divulge the process to any one. In this way a knowledge of it became disseminated, and stereotyping in plaster was generally practically adopted.

——— Stereotype Printing. London : 1811. 8vo.

This is a small tract of eight leaves addressed "to the Public," against the combination of London Booksellers to ruin Wilson's stereotype publications.

WILSON (F. J. F.).- Stereotyping and Electrotyping. A Guide for the Production of Plates by the Papier-Mâché and Plaster Processes, with Instructions for Depositing Copper by the Battery or by the Dynamo-machine. Also Hints on Steel and Brassfacing, &c. London : [1882]. 12mo. pp. xv. 195.

Undoubtedly the best English work on these two important accessory processes to the art of Printing. The Introduction consists of a History of Stereotyping, by Mr. John Southward, which, in the words of the preface, presents "a more complete and connected narrative of the origin of the art than has yet appeared, the materials being obtained partly from original sources and partly from researches made at the British Museum and other great libraries." In compiling the work, it is also pointed out in the Preface, "the author of the practical portion has enjoyed peculiar advantages owing to his connexion with one of the most extensive stereotyping and electrotyping establishments in this country (Cassell & Co., Limited)." Obsolete methods have been omitted, while due prominence has been given to those of latest introduction and of greatest practical utility. There is, first of all, presented an account of the Paper process, from making the flong to finishing the plate. Then follows the Plaster process. Electrotyping is next treated of, preceded by an historical account of the invention, also by Mr. Southward. In this, the various experiments and improvements made in the art of electro-metallurgy, from the time of Galvani and Volta up to the invention of the dynamo-electric machine, are succinctly narrated. The process of electrotyping, from taking the mould in wax to trimming and mounting the plate, is described with a degree of detail and lucidity that leaves nothing to impede the student in acquiring the art. The modern processes of etching for copperplate printing, and steel, iron, and brass facing, are subsequently explained. There are many illustrations of machines and apparatus interspersed throughout the work.

———— Typographic Printing **Machines and Machine-Printing.** A Practical Guide to the Selection of Bookwork, Two-colour, Jobbing, and Rotary Machines, with Remarks upon their Construction, Capabilities, and Peculiarities, and Instructions in Making-ready, the Preparation of Engravings, &c. London: [1879]. 12mo. pp. xvi. 202.————Second edition [1882].———— Third edition [1884]. pp. xvi, 208, and Appendix of six pages (pp. 209-214).

It is stated in the Preface that, at the time this hand-book was originally planned, no modern practical work on the same subject existed. The want, it may be mentioned here, has not even yet been supplied, as far as a book in the English language is concerned, the nearest approach being Noble's "Difficulties in Machine Printing, and How to Overcome them," which may be recommended as a supplement to this book, but it does not describe the varieties and construction of machines. In France and Germany, however, several valuable practical works of a very complete character have since appeared (*see* MONNET and WALDOW).

Mr. Wilson's book begins with an account of the distinction between the press and the machine, and of the invention of the latter. This historical part now requires modification, owing to the researches of Herr Theodor Goebel, embodied in his memoir of "Friedrich Koenig und die Erfindung der Schnellpresse" (Stuttgart, 1883), and the valuable articles reviewing it, by Mr. William Blades, in the *Printer's Register*, October, 1883, to June, 1884, inclusive. Mr. Wilson proceeds to give instructions for making-ready, and then enters into particulars of platen, perfecting, single-cylinder, two-colour, jobbing, and rotary machines, not omitting motors, gas, steam, and water engines, concluding with the appliances of the printer's warehouse. In the Appendix of 1884, reference is made to several material changes which, in the short space of five years, had taken place with regard to machine-printing, such as the demand on the part of the public for a higher class of work, the increased strength of the apparatus, the gradual abandonment of large platen machines, the spread of the plan of packing the cylinder with hard material, and the disuse of blankets. The entire work is very carefully done, and forms the most valuable guide to this branch of letter-press printing hitherto produced, especially as it embraces many important hints derived from the practical experience of the author.

Mr. FRED. JOHN FARLOW WILSON is the son of Mr. J. Farlow Wilson, practical manager of the great firm of Cassell & Co., Limited, La Belle Sauvage-yard, Ludgate-hill, a position which he holds owing not less to his administrative abilities than to his capabilities as a practical printer. Brought up under the care and training of a gentleman who was enabled to put his son through the various departments of a first-class establishment, Mr. F. J. F. Wilson learned his business in the most thorough manner by working in each branch for a sufficiently long period to acquire a good technical knowledge of the whole. He then assisted for some time in the details of management. In January, 1880, he obtained the appointment of manager of the extensive printing department of W. H. Smith & Sons, Water-lane, Strand, a situation he has shown himself eminently qualified to fulfil. His opportunities were exceptional, and it is satisfactory to find that he has made such excellent use of them. Both of the works cited above have had a large circulation among English-speaking printers in all parts of the world.

WILSON (John). A Treatise on English Punctuation; designed for Letter-writers, Printers, and Correctors of the Press, and for the use of Schools and Academies. With an Appendix, containing Rules on the use of Capitals, a list of Abbreviations, hints on the Preparation of Copy and on Proof-reading, Specimens of Proof-sheets, &c. Boston: 1850. 16mo.

———— Twenty-third edition. New York : 1871. 8vo. pp. xii. 334.

The first edition, intended solely for the use of Printers, was issued in 1826 ; second edition, 1850 ; third edition, 1855. A very useful and comprehensive work.

WILSON (J. S.). Autotypie. De Natuur zich zelve afbeeldende. Meppel : 1857. Oblong.

WILSON (W.). The Compositor's Assistant, containing all the Imposition Tables now in use. Exeter : 1855.

WIMPHELING [or WIMFELING] (Jacob). Oratio in Memoriam Marsilii ab Inghen. Mainz : 1499.

Several extracts relating to printing are reprinted in Wolf, "Monumenta Typographica." Jacob Wimpheling, says De Vinne ("Invention of Printing," page 393), was one of the most learned men of his age, and nearly contemporary with Gutenberg. He says that in 1440, under the reign of Frederick III., Emperor of the Romans, John Gutenberg, of Strasbourg, discovered a new method of writing, which is a great good, &c. He was the first in the city of Strasbourg who invented that art of impressing which the Latin peoples call printing. He afterwards went to Mentz, and happily perfected his invention. In another book, says De Vinne, he writes : "Your city [Strasbourg] is acknowledged to excel most other cities by its origination of the art of printing, which was afterwards perfected in Mentz." Hessels, on the other hand, discredits this author. He says (p. 118), "This scholar, who wrote occasionally on the invention of printing, was the editor of the Heidelburg professors, and added, by way of amusement, the epitaph of Adam Gelthus and his own epigram."—*See* HESSELS, "Gutenberg."

WINARICKY (Charles). Jean Gutenberg, né en 1412 à Kuttenberg en Bohême, Bachelier-ès-Arts à l'Université de Prague, promu le 18 Novembre 1445, inventeur de l'imprimerie à Mayence en 1450. Essai historique et critique, traduit du manuscrit allemand par Jean de Carro. Bruxelles : 1847. 8vo. pp. 104.

These pages go to prove the usual account of Gutenberg's parentage erroneous, and that he was born at Kuttenberg, a small town in Bohemia.

———— *See* DE VINNE.

WINCKLER (Dr. Johann). Die periodische Presse Oesterreichs. Eine historisch-statistische Studie. Wien : 1875. 8vo.

This work consists of 234 pages of historical and descriptive, and 222 pages of tabular matter, giving an exhaustive picture of the periodical press in Austria, from its beginning up to the time of the publication of the book.

WINTERFELD (C. van). Dr. Martin Luthers deutsche geistliche Lieder, nebst den während seines Lebens dazu gebräuchlichen Singweisen und einigen mehrstimmigen Vorsätzen über dieselben, von Meistern des 16. Jahrhunderts. Herausgegeben als Festschrift für die iv. Jubelfeier der Erfindung der Buchdruckerkunst. Leipzig 1840. 4to. 1 leaf. pp. 132, with woodcuts drawn by A. Strähuber.

WIPPEL (J. F.). Abhandlung über die Formschneidekunst. Breslau : 1879. 4to.

VOL. III.　　　　N

BASLE: 1535-40.

WINTER (Robert).

    The device, above, of this printer consists of Minerva standing in a bower, a lance in her left hand, and leaning with the other on the shield with Medusa's head ; the owl opposite the shield.

WINTER (W.).   Types : an article in the *Atlantic Monthly*, vol. 13. Boston : 1864.   8vo.

WITTIG (C. F.) and FISCHER (C. F.).   Die Schnellpresse, ihre Mechanik und Vorrichtung zum Druck aller typographischen Arbeiten. Leipzig : 1878.   8vo.   pp. iii. 105.   (1st edition, 1861 ; 2nd edition, 1866.)

    This technical manual treats more particularly of the printing-machines manufactured at the Augsburg factory.

WITZLEBEN (C. D. von). Geschichte der *Leipziger Zeitung.* Zur Erinnerung an das 200-jährige Bestehen dieser Zeitung. Leipzig. 1860.   8vo.   pp. vi. 218.

WITZSCH (Joh. Chr.). Brauch und Missbrauch der edlen Buch-druckerkunst, als Herr Joh. Georg Witzsch dieser löblichen Kunst bissher Beflissener den 25. Mai Anno 1722 bey Verschenckung seines Postulats in die Zahl rechtschaffener Kunst-Verwandten in Altenburg aufgenommen wurde. Altenburg : 1722. Folio.

WOELLMER]. Schriftproben von Wilh Woellmer's Schriftgiesserei in Berlin (Madrid, St. Petersburg, London, Paris). 1879. 4to. 22 double sheets. s.d.
Several continuations have since been published.

WOERL (Leon). Die katholische Presse in Europa, 1877. 2nd edition. Würzburg 1877. 8vo. pp. 188. 4 leaves. (1st edition 1876.)

[———] Die Publicistik der Gegenwart. Eine Rundschau über die gesammte Presse der Welt. :—Part I., Hessen-Baden : 1879. 16mo. pp. 87. Part II., Württemberg : 1879. Part III., Schweizerische Eidgenossenschaft 1879. Part IV., Oesterreich. Ungarn, 1881. Part V., Preussen, 1881. Würzburg : 1879-81. 16mo. pp. 1113.

——— Statistik der katholischen Zeitungen und Zeitschriften in der ganzen Welt zu Neujahr 1879. Würzburg : 1879. pp. 62. 1 leaf.

[———] Welt-Rundschau über die katholische Presse. Neujahr, 1878. 8vo. 21 sheets. Würzburg : 1878.

WOHLFARTH (A.). Ueber Farben. 2te verb. Auflage. 8vo. 6½ sheets. Mit Spectral-Farben und Farbentafel in 80 Farben. Leipzig : 1882.

WOLF (C. E.). Warum haben wir als evangelische Christen für die Erfindung der Buchdruckerkunst Gott zu danken ? Eine Predigt am zweiten Sonntage nach Trinitatis den 28. Jun. 1840 zum Gedächtniss des vierten Jubelfestes nach der Erfindung der Buchdruckerkunst gehalten. Saalfeld : 8vo. pp. 16.

WOLF (Joh. Christian). Monumenta typographica, quæ artis hujus præstantissimæ originem, laudem et abusum posteris produnt. Hamburgi : 1740. Small 8vo. 2 vols. Vol. I. 8 leaves, pp. 96, 1104. Vol. II. 1 leaf, pp. 1323.

The following treatises are reprinted in these two thick volumes :—

Bergellani (Jo. Arn.) Poëma de Chalco-graphiæ inventione, 1541. [*See* BERGELLANUS.]
Stephani (Henr.) Artis typographicæ querimonia, et Epitaphia Typographorum doctorum, 1569. [*See* STEPHANUS, H.]
Judicis (Matthæ.) Libellus de typographiæ inventione et de praelorum inspectione, 1566. [*See* RICHTER.]
Besoldi (Christoph.) Dissert. de in-ventione Typographiæ, 1620. [*See* BESOLDUS.]
Scriverii (Pet.) Laurea Laurentii Costeri, è belgico, 1628. [*See* SCHRIJVER, P.]
Anonymi (Fausti) Relatio MS. de Origine Typographiæ, è germanico.
Ex Naudaei (Gabr.) Additamentis ad Historiam Ludovici XI., Regis Galliarum, è gallico. [*See* NAUDÉ, G.]
Ex Boxhornii(Marci Zuerii) Theatro urbium Hollandiæ, 1632. [*See* BOXHORN.]
Mallincrot (Bernh.). Dissert. de ortu et progressu artis typographicæ, 1640. [*See* MALLINKROT.]

Boxhornii (Marci Zuerii) Dissert. de typographicæ artis inventione, 1640. [*See* BOXHORN.]

Ejusdem Historia Universali, 1652.

Rivini (Andr.) Hecatomba laudum ob inventam Chalcographiam, 1640. [*See* RIVINUS.]

Ejusdem Oratio de artis Typographicæ præstantia, 1640.

Brehmen (C.). Expositio inventionis artis typographicæ cum carminibus latinis variorum, è germanico, 1640. [*See* BREHM.]

Carmina Secularia de Typographia, cura Ge. Baumanni excusa.

Kleinwechteri (Valent.) Actus Seculares II. in laudem typographiæ, 1640. [*See* KLEINWECHTER.]

Starkii (Sebast. Gottfr.) Oratio de arte typographica, è germanico, 1640. [*See* STARCKE, P.]

Rivini (Andr.) Controversiæ de artis typographicæ inventione, è germanico, 1640. [*See* RIVINUS.]

Gveintzii (Christiani) Encomium artis typographicæ, è germanico, 1640.

Insulani Menapii (Gulielmi) Statera Chalcographiæ, 1547.

Schragii (Jo. Adami) Historia Typographiæ, è germanico. [*See* SCHRAG, J. A.]

Schmidii (Jo.) Conciones III. Eucharisticæ, è germanico, 1640.

Boecleri (Jo. Henr.) Oratio de Typographiæ divinitate, 1641. [*See* BOECLERUS.]

Mentelii (Jac.) Brevis excursus de loco, tempore et auctore inventionis Typographiæ, cum notis MSS., 1644. [*See* MENTELIUS.]

Ejusdem Parænesis de Typographiæ origine, 1650.

Ejusdem Observationes MSS. de Typographis et Typographia.

Gutneri (Jo. Gabr.) Typographiæ Chemnitiensis primæ plagulæ, è germanico, 1661. [*See* GUTNER.]

Fritschii (Ahas.) Dissert. de abusibus Typographiæ tollendis, 1662. [*See* FRITSCH.]

Stohrii (J.) Dissert. de ortu Typographiæ, 1666. [*See* STOHR.]

Vesteri (Christiani) Nobilissima ars typographica descripta, è germanico. [*See* VESTER.]

Fritschii (Ahas.) Dissert. de Typographia, 1675.

Normanni (Laur.) Dissert. de Typographia, 1689. [*See* NORMANNUS.]

Licimandri Panegyricus in laudem artis typographicæ, è germanico, 1690.

Moller (Dan. Guill.). Dissert. de Typographia, 1692. [*See* MOLLER.]

Schroedteri (Ern. Christiani) Dissert. de Typographia. [*See* SCHROEDTER.]

Thiboust (C. Ludov.). Carmen Latinum, 1699. [*See* THIBOUST.]

Tentzelii (Wilh. Ern.) Dissert. de inventione Typographiæ, è germanico, 1700. [*See* TENTZEL.]

Krausii (Jo. Christoph.) Laudes Typographiæ, è germanico, 1709. [*See* KRAUS.]

Patris (Pauli) Dissert. de Typis Literarum, 1710. [*See* PATER.]

Fekno (Pet. Paul). Programma de typographia et pulvere pyrio, 1713. [*See* FEKNO.]

Oudini (Casim.) Dissert. de primis artis typographicæ inventoribus, 1722. [*See* OUDIN.]

Tolandi (J.) Conjectura de Typographiæ inventione, 1722. [*See* TOLAND.]

Natolini (Jo. Bap.) Dissert. de arte imprimendi, ex italico, 1607. [*See* NATOLINI.]

Catherinot (Nic.). Ars imprimendi, è Gallico, 1685. [*See* CATHERINOT.]

Bockenhofferi (Jr. Phil.) Brevis relatio, è danico, 1691. [*See* BOCKENHOFFER.]

Observationes de ortu et progressu Typographiæ, ex anglico, 1703.

Bagfordi (Jo.) Exercitatio de inventione Typographiæ, ex anglico, 1707. [*See* BAGFORD.]

Loca selecta et carmina variorum.

Wolf's book is, in itself as well as in its contents, a "typographical monument." He collected many fugitive and ephemeral dissertations, poems, memoirs, &c., and translated them into Latin. In this way he has preserved some of the literature of printing that might otherwise have passed away into oblivion. The pieces are, of course, of unequal value ; some, indeed having no value at all as history, but as curiosities. In this BIBLIOGRAPHY most of them have been cited under the names of their authors, and the annotations given may be useful to students of this remarkable collection.

In part i., vol. i., is the first Bibliography of Printing ever compiled. It is headed :— "Bibliotheca Typographica, seu elenchus scriptorum, qui partem copiosę, partem breviter, artem typographicum illustrarunt" (pp. 1–72). There are brief annotations to many of the items.

JOHANN CHRISTIAN VON WOLF was a German philosopher and mathematician, born 1679; was named professor of mathematics at Halle, in 1707. Through the influence, partly of personal enemies, and partly of the "odium theologicum," he was deprived of his chair and banished from Prussia, 1723. He long held the chair of mathematics and philosophy at Marburg ; but on the invitation of Frederick the Great he returned to Halle, in 1741, as professor of international law. His chief philosophical work is entitled " Philosophia Rationalis," which appeared in 1728, followed by " Philosophia Prima," "Theologica Naturalis," and several others.

It is important to observe that John Christian Wolf, the author of the above, had a brother, John Christopher Wolf (*see infra*), as the similarity of names has led to confusion.

WOLF (John Christopher). Conspectus supellectilis epistolicæ et litterariæ manu exaratæ quæ exstat apud Jo. Christoph. Wolfium. Hamburg : 1736. 8vo.

JOHN CHRISTOPHER WOLF was the brother of John Christian Wolf, who compiled the "Monumenta Typographica " (*see supra*). He was a pastor of a congregation at Hamburg, and made a large collection of manuscripts and publications, many having reference to the origin of printing. Some of these he bought from the heirs of Zacharias Conrad von Uffenbach, a distinguished magistrate and collector of literary treasures at Frankfurt, who died in 1734. A number of references to this writer and his monuments will be found in Hessels' "Gutenberg."

WOLF (Dr. Carl). Schriftproben der Buchdruckerey von. München : 1825. 4to.

WOLF (Lucien). Exhibition and Market of Machinery, Implements, and Material used by Printers, etc. Official Catalogue of Exhibits. London : 1880. 8vo. pp. 290.

—— Second Annual Exhibition and Market, etc. London : 1881. 8vo. pp. 208.

—— Third Printers', Stationers', Papermakers', and Fine Art Exhibition and Market. London : 1883. 8vo. pp. 160.

The catalogue of three exhibitions of machinery, materials, and products, held in the Agricultural Hall, Islington, London, in 1880, 1881, and 1883 respectively. The originator and organiser was Mr. Robert Dale, who was connected with the management of the great hall, originally built for the purpose of periodical cattle shows. Mr. Dale's idea was that an exhibition of the kind would be useful for advertising and business purposes to those who contributed to it, and interesting to the public, who would be attracted to it. His idea was only partially realised. The first exhibition was a very good one, and there was a large attendance. It was under the patronage of the Lord Mayor of London, Sir Francis Wyatt Truscott; the Lord Mayor of Dublin, the Rt. Hon. E. Dwyer Grey, M.P.; the Lord Provost of Edinburgh, the Rt. Hon. Thos. J. Boyd ; and the Lord Provost of Glasgow, the Rt. Hon. Wm. Collins, for it was a singular coincidence that in this year the chief magistrates of the chief cities in the kingdom were printers, stationers, or publishers. A charge was made for the space room occupied by exhibitors, and there was also a charge for admission to visitors. The second exhibition was arranged on much the same lines ; but there was a falling off in the number, both of exhibitors and visitors. A year was allowed to pass by, and then a third exhibition took place. Mr. Dale had been warned that the period intervening between these exhibitions was too small, and several leading firms announced that they would refrain from taking any part in the matter. Mr. Dale, however, had announced his intention, and could not be prevailed upon to relinquish it. The result was that the exhibition was a great falling-off even upon its predecessor. Mr. Dale died in January of the following year, aged 40. He was a man of great energy, business capacity, urbanity, and uprightness.

In addition to the list and a classified catalogue of the exhibits, the first catalogue contains a preface, and an article on "The Future of Trade Exhibitions," by the editor. Then followed a long article on "The Origin and Progress of Printing," by Mr. John Southward. It was divided into short histories of the printing - press, composition rollers, motors, typefounding, stereotyping, electrotyping, type - setting, pressing printed sheets, engraving on metal, en-

graving on wood, process blocks, glycerine tablets, and lithography. As might
be expected from an author engaged for
many years in writing continuously for
the trade journals, the information was
brought up to date and accurate. Future
historians may find it of use as denoting
the processes in vogue in the year 1880.

The catalogue of the second exhibition
contained a preface, and articles on
display letterpress (jurors, Messrs. J.
Collingridge, C. Hayman, and J. Southward). There were also competitions
for various kinds of jobbing work, and
in distributing and composing a certain
quantity of type in the pres-nce of visitors.
A new lay of the case, and regulations
to prevent unfairness and fraud, were
drawn up by Mr. Southward. This com-
petition was watched with great interest.

LONDON : 1579-1600.

printing machinery and appliances, &c.,
by the editor. The latter were extremely
slight and of no technical value whatever, the writer not claiming to be a
practical man.

The third catalogue contained only a
general preface. This exhibition was
interesting by its including several competitions, such as for lithographic machines, a locking-up column galley,
locking-up apparatus, and high-art
The result, showing the speed at which
the best picked hands can work for a
given time, is recorded in the *British and
Colonial Printer and Stationer*, October
11, 1883.

Medals were struck to commemorate
the first and second exhibitions. These
medals are described in Mr. W. Blades's
" Numismata Typographica " (London,
1883. 4to.).

WOLFE (John).

JOHN WOLFE (see device on p. 94) was a city printer and also a fishmonger. Stow, in his "Survey," gives a curious account of him. "He used the art of printing, and in a contest between the patentees and the Stationers' Company, taking upon him as a captain in this cause, was content with no agreement, but generally affirmed that he might and would print any lawful book, notwith-standing the commandment of the queen. And to that end had incensed the popularity of London, as in a common cause, somewhat dangerously. And with him several of the rest changing their minds were associated, and laboured to over-throw those privileges the queen had granted, or could grant. Whereupon the above said committees of the Stationers' Company, finding them so disordered, would have bound them to appear before the queen's council, which they promised to do; but after conference with their abettors, refused; and still prosecuted their complaints to her majesty, gar-nishing the same with pretences of the liberties of London, and the common wealth of the said company; and saying the queen was deceived by those that were the means for obtaining such privi-leges." Wolfe was afterwards in such favour with the citizens that he was made printer to the City of London. He dwelt at Paul's Chain and in Distaff-lane, over against the sign of the Castle, and had a shop in Pope's-head-alley, and in Lombard-street, in 1598. The device is the fleur-de-lys seeding; with the legend "ubique floret." John Wolfe was City printer in 1581, and was succeeded by John Windet.

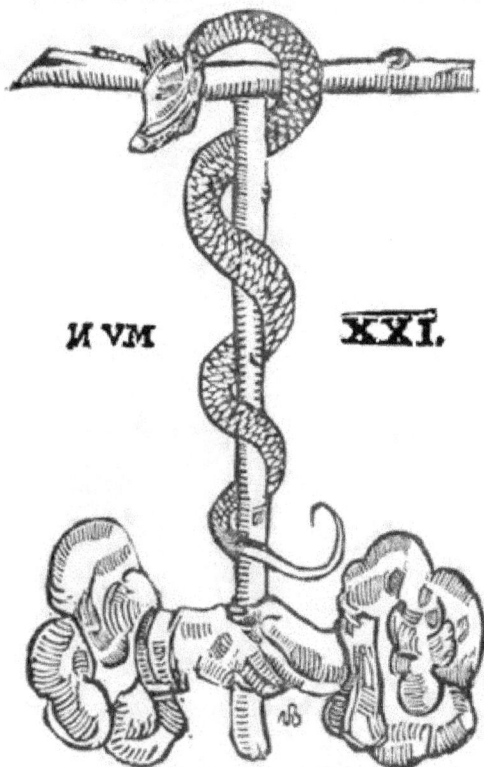

ИVM   XXI.

LONDON : 1542-1573.

WOLFE (Reynold).

Towards the latter part of the fifteenth century there were several printers of this name: as George Wolfe, of Baden, who printed at Paris from 1491 to 1499; Nicholas Wolfe, at Lyons, in 1498 and 1499; Nicholas a learned man, a good antiquary, a great promoter of the Reformation, and that he enjoyed the favour of Henry VIII., Cromwell, Earl of Essex, Archbishop Cranmer, and others. He spent twenty-five years in collecting materials for a "Universal Cos-

Wolfe, a German, in 1502; and Thomas Wolfe, at Basle, in 1527. It is probable that Reynold or Reginald Wolfe, who was King's Printer, was related to one or more of them, and was of foreign extraction. It is, however, certain that he was mogony," which, though left unarranged at his death, formed the foundation of Holinshed's "Chronicles," as is stated in the dedication. It was Stow's intention, had he lived another year, to have printed Reynold Wolfe's "Chronicle,"

which was begun and finished by desire of Whitgift, Archbishop of Canterbury. Wolfe's printing-office stood in St. Paul's-churchyard, at the sign of the Brazen Serpent, which emblem he used as a device. Stow thought that he built his dwelling "from the ground, out of the old chapel which he purchased of the king at the dissolution of the monasteries; on the same ground he had several other tenements, and afterwards purchased several leases of the dean and chapter of St. Paul's." He followed his typographical occupation for some years with great reputation; he printed most of Archbishop Cranmer's writings, and was also employed by other eminent men. Ames says that he was the first person who enjoyed a patent for being printer to the king in Latin, Greek, and Hebrew; by which instrument he was also authorised to be his majesty's bookseller and stationer, with an annuity of 26s. 8d. during life. All other booksellers and stationers were prohibited from printing or selling any of his books. During Queen Mary's reign Ames supposes that Wolfe was employed in preparing the materials which compose Holinshed's "Chronicle." In the first year of the reign of Elizabeth, he became Master of the Stationers' Company, to which he was a generous benefactor and one of the original members.

In 1564, 1567, and 1572, he again served the same office. He is thought to have died in 1573, when he was buried in the church of St. Faith.

The portrait herewith is that drawn by Faithorne, and reprinted in Ames's "Typographical Antiquities." Wolfe used two devices, the larger one of which is here reproduced. It was probably adopted from some foreign printer, as the serpent was usually introduced in their devices. "This, perhaps," says Johnson in the "Typographia," "came from Conrad Neobanus (*vide* his 'Apostolorum et Sanctorum Concilia,' 1510, 4to). There appears to have been some tangible figure of this device, probably a carved sign, since in the will of Wolfe's widow the Brazen Serpent is a part of the goods bequeathed to her other son Robert. Wolfe's other device, of which there are two sizes, consisted of an elegant cartouche German shield, on which is represented a fruit-tree and two boys, one of whom is taking down the fruit with a stick, whilst the other is taking it up off the ground. A large scroll of two folds passes between the upper branches of the tree containing the word "Charitas" in small Roman characters; whence this device is called by Ames and Herbert the "Tree of Charity."

WOLFF (II.). Die Schwierigkeiten der Correctoren u. Drucker. In Herrig's "Archives Belgiques," xxiii. pp. 451.

WOLFFGER (Georg). Neu-auffgesetztes Format-Büchlein, oder Vorgestellte Nachrichtungs-Figuren wie man auff der löblichen Kunst Buch-Druckerey in allen gross- vnd kleinen Formaten die Columnen recht ordentlich ausschiessen vnd stellen soll : Mit nothwendigem Unterricht in Abtheilung der halben Bögen 3. Th. 4. Th. 6. Th. &c. Allen Kunst-Verwandten zu nutzlichen Gebrauch gesetzt und gedruckt worden Anno Christi M.DC.LXXIII. Graz. Oblong 8vo.

Thirty leaves, twenty-one of which are numbered. This is a most interesting and curious book of plans of impositions, giving also figures of a Press and all a Printer's working tools, by the use of brass-rule and types only, with great skill; the whole being composed in leisure-time and holidays. The author was a compositor in the "Widmanstetterischen Druckerey," and finished his schemes of imposition in 1670, when he set up the following title-page for them:— "Neu-auffgesetztes Format-Büchlein, darinnen abgesetzte Figuren, wie man die Columnen ausschiessen soll,

in allen gemeinen Formaten [*sic*], mit sambt deren Abtheilungen. Allen der löblichen Buchdruckerey-Kunst Erfahrnen, besonders denen Setzer-Gesellen, vnd Lehrjungen gantz nutzlich vnd beförderlich zu gebrauchen, weilen es nicht alles im Gedächtnuss kan behalten werden. In der Landsfürstlichen Haupt-Stadt Grätz in den Druck gegeben, von Georgen Wolffger, B.G. 1670." He appears to have occupied two years in completing the curious designs for the additional pages, and then to have reprinted his title-page in 1673, as above.

VOL. III. O

WOLTMANN (Dr. Alfred). **Geschichte** der Deutschen **Kunst** im Elsass. Leipzig 1876. 8vo. pp. xvi. 330. 74 illustrations.

A history of German art architecture, painting, &c., in Alsace. A considerable part of the work is devoted to the subject of early wood-engraving in Strasbourg, and there are many choice specimens reproduced in facsimile.

WOOD (A. A.). Popular Lectures for the Magic Lantern : The History of Printing. London : [1870]. 8vo.

WOOD (James). Specimens of Printing-Types for Book, Newspaper, and General Work. London : [1875]. 8vo.

WOOD & Co. The New French Mode of Stereotyping. A broadside.

WOOD & SHARWOODS. The Specimen Book of Types cast at the Austin Letter Foundry. London : 1839 and 1844. 4to.

About the early part of the present century, one of the well-known foundries was that of Richard Austin, situated in Worship-street, Finsbury. He was followed by his son George Austin (as Austin & Son in 1824), a very clever punch cutter. The foundry was afterwards bought by R. M. Wood, the elder, a typefounder. Subsequently he was joined by Sharwoods, Samuel and Thomas, the foundry being carried on at 120, Aldersgate-street, also the manufacture of printing material. Wood died September 28, 1845, aged 38. The foundry was then carried on by the two Sharwoods. After the death of the last surviving member of the Sharwoods, Thomas, the foundry was thrown into Chancery. It subsequently passed to two sons of R. M. Wood, named J. and R. M. Wood. They removed it from Aldersgate-street to 89, West Smithfield, and thence to Farringdon-road, and here carried on business besides as printers' brokers, manufacturers of materials, also publishing the *Typographic Advertiser.* R. M. Wood had two other sons, who became typefounders, in Islington. They bought, in 1849, the plant of Geo. Williamson, typefounder, Parkfield-street, and greatly added to it by electrotyping matrices. Austin Wood died February 21, 1883, aged 43. His brother Rowland now carries on the business.

The Islington firm claim that it was Austin Wood who modified the old style Roman to the present ; the other branch of the family claim that it was George Austin. We are not able to settle the doubt, as the firm of Austin Wood & Co. refuse any information.

WOODBERRY (George E.). A History of Wood-Engraving. New York : 1883. 4to. pp. xii. 221. 90 woodcut illustrations.

A popular treatise. The illustrations are specimens in facsimile of wood-engravings from the earliest period, and from the original blocks of recent artists.

WOODCOCK (Thomas).

THOMAS WOODCOCK was a London stationer and bookseller, who lived in St. Paul's-churchyard, at the sign of the Black Bess. He married Isabel, the second daughter of John Cawood, a celebrated printer in his day. The device on p. 99, is a very good example of the punning rebus, a cock on a wood heap, with the motto, " Cantabo Jehovæ quia benefecit." The date is that given in Berjeau's " Printers' Marks," from which the engraving is copied. Other authorities state that Woodcock was in business from 1575 to 1591.

[WOODCROFT]. Abridgments of Specifications relating to Letterpress and similar printing (excluding Electro-telegraphic and Photographic Printing). Part ii., 1867–1876. Printed by order of the Commissioners of Patents. London : 1880. 8vo. pp. xii. 586.

Under the heading PATENT OFFICE PUBLICATIONS is given a list of the Abstracts of Specifications relating to Printing, &c., as issued up to the date of publication of the second volume of this BIBLIOGRAPHY. Since then the Part ii., 1858 to 1866, has been officially catalogued as Ia, and another volume, to be known as Part ii. has been issued, bringing up the Abstracts to 1876, as above noted. The preface is signed by H. Reader Lack, and except in regard to the idea of the work, no part is attributable to Mr. Woodcroft. We avail ourselves of the name, however, to give a complete list of these issues.

LONDON: 1570-1594.

WOODEN PRINTING PRESS of the Original Construction. London: November, 1863. Broadside.

The following quotation explains itself:—The Press referred to is in the Museum of Patents at South Kensington:—"As a matter of some literary interest, it may be mentioned that this Press was removed from the office of Messrs. Cox & Wyman in Great Queen-street (now almost the oldest printing-house in London), where it occupied the site of that at which the celebrated Dr. Franklin worked in 1725-6, when he followed the calling of a journeyman printer. It resembles the 'Franklin Press,' of which, though not quite so ancient, it was a contemporary, and it is possible that it was worked occasionally by the celebrated American philosopher.

The 'Franklin Press' passed from the printing-office in Great Queen-street into the hands of Messrs. Harrild & Son, of London, and it is now a cherished object in the Museum of the American Philosophical Society of Philadelphia.

Application having been made by the Patent Office Museum to its possessor, Mr. Charles Wyman, this press was at once kindly presented by that gentleman to Her Majesty's Commissioners."

WORKING-MAN'S WAY IN THE WORLD (The) : being the Auto-
biography of a Journeyman Printer. London : [1854]. 8vo.
pp. xii. 347.

—— *See* SMITH (Charles Manby).

WORKS relating to Bibliography, History of Printing, Bookbinding,
&c. Catalogue of Public Libraries on Sale. Oxford 1880.
8vo. pp. 62.

WORTE, noch einige, über Büchernachdruck. Pappenheim : 1823. 8vo.

WRIGHT (James). Country Conversations, chiefly of the Modern
Comedies, of Drinking, of Translated Verse, of Printing and
Printers, of Poets and Poetry. London : 1694. 12mo.

JAMES WRIGHT, the antiquary, was born about 1644 : died about 1715.

WUNDER (Moritz). Ueber Preisberechnung von Druckarbeiten.
Leipzig. 1885. 8vo. pp. 56.

A treatise on the calculations of the prices charged for printing books, jobs, &c.,
giving tables, schedules, and other information.

WÜRDTWEIN (Etienne Alexander). Bibliotheca Moguntina libris
saeculo primo typographico Moguntiae impressis instructa, hinc
inde addita inventae typographiae historia. Augustae Vindel. :
1789. 4to. pp. 251, with 9 plates.

Some curious plates of facsimile. ETIENNE ALEXANDER WÜRDTWEIN, a scholar of Worms, published a work of great interest on the origin of printing. It was entitled " Bibliotheca Moguntina" (Augsbourg, 1787, 4to.). The author treats with considerable minuteness of the genealogy of Gutenberg, of Fust, and of Peter Schoeffer, and engraves their arms and crests. He has copied, with the utmost veri-similitude, the colophons of all the early Mayence editions to which he could obtain access. Especially admirable is his facsimile of portions of the Psalter of 1457, which reproduces in exact size all the peculiarities of the original, as well as the system of abbreviation and punctuation adopted. Hessels ("Gutenberg") makes repeated references to this work, and shows its untrustworthiness in several places.

WURM (Prof.). Festrede zur Jubelfeier der Buchdruckerkunst in
Hamburg am 24. Juni, 1840. 8vo. (Auch abgedruckt im Börsen-
blatt f.d. deutschen Buchhandel 1840. No. 81-82.)

WURSTEISEN (Christ.). Kurzer Begriff der Geschichte von Basel,
aus dem Latein übersetzt und mit Anmerkungen vermehret von
Jac. Christ. Beck. Basel : 1757. 8vo. (Pp. 209, 210, 217-219 :
Ueber den Anfang der Buchdruckerkunst in Basel und die dortigen
berühmten Buchdrucker.)

WURTH-PAQUET (Fr.). Typographie Luxembourgeoise. (Dans le
Bulletin de la Société pour la Recherche et la Conservation des
Monuments historiques dans le Grand Duché de Luxembourg,
1850.)

WURZBACH (Dr. Alfred von). Martin Schongauer. Eine kritische
Untersuchung seines Lebens und seiner Werke, nebst einem
chronologischen Verzeichnisse seiner Kupferstiche. Wien : 1880.
8vo. pp. iv. 124, and leaf of contents.

WÜSTEMANN (E. F.). Oratio in quartis inventæ artis Gutenbergianæ solemnibus sæcularibus quæ eadem secunda fuerunt, officinæ Typographicæ in urbe Gotha conditæ sacra secularia. Gothæ : 1840. 8vo. pp. 22.

WUSTMANN (Dr. G.). Die Anfänge des Leipziger Bücherwesens. für iv. Saecularfeier der Einführung der Buchdruckerei in Leipzig, 1479. Leipzig : 1879. 8vo. pp. 23.

Reprinted from the " Archiv. für Geschichte des Buchhandels."

———— Illustrirter Weihnachts-Catalog für den deutschen Buchhandel. Leipzig : 8vo.

To this catalogue, which is still published every year, a literary review is added, written by Dr. Wustmann, secretary of the Town Library at Leipzig during the years 1870 to 1877. He has treated his subject with great ability and competence, not only from a literary, but also from a typographical point of view.

———— Luther's Bibeldrucker. In the "Grenzboten." Leipzig : 1878. No. 34.

WUTTKE (Dr. Heinrich). Geschichte der Schrift und des Schrifttums, von den rohen Anfängen des Schreibens in der Tatuirung, bis zur Legung elektromagnetischer Dräthe. Erster Band : Die verschiedenen Schriftsysteme. Leipzig : 1872. 8vo. pp. xxiv. 782. With an Atlas of xxxiii. plates, and 25 pp. of explanations.

Only one volume of this scientific and highly valuable work has appeared ; the author died in 1876, before the second volume was ready for print. He shows that the art of Printing,—that is, the art of impressing by means of certain forms and colours, figures, pictures, letters, words, lines, whole pages, &c., on other objects,—existed long before the fifteenth century. In Nineveh, centuries before our era, the strokes of cuneated letters were impressed without any difficulty in soft clay by means of a graver; the Babylonians cut the same characters in relief on wooden blocks, in order to impress them by these means in wet clay.

———— Die deutschen Zeitschriften und die Entstehung der öffentlichen Meinung. Ein Beitrag zur Geschichte des Zeitungswesens. Dritte Auflage. Leipzig : 1875. 8vo. pp. 448.

This book, giving a history of the Press in Germany, is a most remarkable one. As it reveals the many weak points of the daily papers and their editors in a most pitiless manner, its author had to suffer many enmities, and his book was torn to pieces by the offended critics ; still it went rapidly from edition to edition, and the author was just preparing its fourth, when death overtook him.

———— Le Journalisme allemand et la formation de l'opinion publique en Allemagne. Trad. sur la 3ᵐᵉ édit. avec l'autoris. de l'auteur par R. Pommerol. Paris : 1876. 18mo. pp. xxvi. 296.

WYMAN (Charles William Henry). In Memoriam Charles Wyman. London : 1878. 8vo. pp. 4.

An obituary memoir of Mr. Charles Wyman (father of the writer), head of the firm of Wyman & Sons. Mr. Wyman had, in early youth, chosen the nautical profession ; but, circumstances leading him to become a printer, he was apprenticed to Mr. William Shackell, proprietor of the *John Bull* newspaper. The printing-office was in Johnson's-court, Fleet-street, and its owner resided, with some of his apprentices, in Gough-square, close by. Mr. Shackell was a master of the old-fashioned school, and insisted upon his apprentices being taught their trade with a thoroughness somewhat rare at the present day. A very stringent interpretation of his rights as an employer led to a rebellion on the part of Charles Wyman, who finished the remainder of his time as an outdoor apprentice; but the quarrel was subsequently healed, and both parties, for many years, held each other in mutual esteem. Having mastered the duties of the reading-closet, Mr. Wyman became overseer at the office of Mr. W. M'Dowall, 4, Pemberton-row, a classical scholar and a very able printer. He relinquished this position in July, **1840**, to take control of the office of Messrs. Cox & Sons, the famous Oriental printers.

Gifted with much force of character and indomitable energy, Mr. Wyman soon imparted a new impulse to the old concern, from which, after a while, Mr. John Lewis Cox, its chief, retired, in favour of his sons John and Henry, who subsequently entered into partnership with Mr. Wyman. The style of the firm was then altered to Cox (Bros.) and Wyman. After the death of Mr. Henry Cox, and the retirement of Mr. John Cox in the year 1858 in favour of his mother (who only lived a few months after her partnership with Mr. Wyman), the style of the firm became Cox & Wyman, and this again was altered to Wyman & Sons after Mr. Wyman

acquired sole possession of the business. When he took control at Great Queen-street the establishment could only boast of a solitary double-demy Napier machine, and even that was turned by hand, but gradually and steadily its resources were developed. He succeeded to the important appointment of Printer to the Honourable East India Company, an office which he held until its abolition by the transfer of the Company's rights to the Crown.

In 1866 Mr. Wyman retired in favour of his eldest son, Charles William Henry (one of the compilers of this BIBLIOGRAPHY), and his youngest surviving son, Edward F., who had long been associated with their father in Great Queen-street. Mr. Wyman was an occasional contributor to the Press, and a speaker of more than average ability. Thoroughly versed in the intricacies of the printing business, his judgment was frequently sought in trade difficulties. When a young man he was president of the Readers' Association, and later on a member of the committee of the Master-Printers' Association. He died at his residence, Broadlands, South Norwood, on February 27, 1878, aged seventy-four years, and was buried in the family grave at Highgate Cemetery.

———— List of Technical **Terms** relating to **Printing** Machinery. Compiled by the editor of the *Printing Times and Lithographer.* London : 1882. 8vo. pp. 80.

The first list of the technical words and expressions used in the machine-room. The terminology of this comparatively new and important branch of the Printing business is interesting, many of the words being adapted colloquialisms, and others abbreviations or corruptions of mechanical and scientific words.

CHARLES WILLIAM HENRY WYMAN was born in 1832, and was duly apprenticed to the Printing business in the above-mentioned office of Messrs. Cox. From the completion of his apprenticeship he took an active part in the

superintendence of this large concern, and, on becoming one of the partners, undertook the control of the practical details of the business, his younger brother, Edward F. Wyman, having charge of the commercial and financial department. Mr. C. W. H. Wyman largely interested himself in the "politics" of the trade, and was successively vice-chairman and chairman of the London Master Printers' Association ; he also took an active part in the affairs of the Printers' Pension Corporation. (*See supra*, and *Printing Times and Lithographer, s.v.* PERIODICAL PUBLICATIONS.)

WYMAN'S TECHNICAL SERIES.—*See* BEADNELL (Spelling and Punctuation) ; RICHMOND (Grammar of Lithography) ; SOUTHWARD (Authorship and Publication); WILSON (Printing Machines, Stereotyping and Electrotyping). Among other works published by the firm are Colour and Colour Printing as applied to Lithography, by W. D. Richmond (author of the "Grammar of Lithography") ; the *Printing Trades' Diary (see* PERIODICAL PUBLICATIONS), and *Everybody's Year-Book*—the issue of which for 1877 contained "Four Centuries of Printing in England,"

and many chronological facts, in the Calendar. relating to typo-graphy and the accessory arts. The issue for 1868 contained "A History of Great Queen-street," with an account of the Franklin Press (*see* FRANKLIN, *ante*). Other references to the firm and its publications will be found *s. v. Printing Times and Lithographer* (PERIODICAL PUBLICATIONS). *See also* CHAPEL RULES, *ante*.

WYNKEN DE WORDE. Lady Margaret's Funeral Sermon, by Dr. Fisher. Reproduced by Dr. Hymers, with a facsimile of the original title-page.

WYNKEN DE WORDE was one of the most eminent of our ancient printers, not only from the number of his pub-lications, but also from the typographical excellence which they exhibit. From an examination of the Rolls patents, it appears that he was born in Lorraine, and became a denizen of England in 1496. It has been conjectured that he was an assistant or workman with Caxton before he came to England; he certainly was connected with him at Westminster, and remained so till

ceived from the Countess of Richmond, daughter of the Duke of Somerset and mother of Henry VII. The colophon of a book printed in 1496 shows that he was then still living at Westminster, in Caxton's house. In this office he appears to have continued until the year 1499, and soon after he removed to "the sign of the Golden Sun," in the parish of St. Bride, in the "Fletestreet." This neigh-bourhood he appears never to have left, and in his will he directs his body to be buried in the parochial church of St.

Caxton's death, about 1496. After this he practised the art of Printing on his own account; perhaps in his master's house. The exact date of his first production is uncertain; Dibdin says it was not before 1493. He also thinks that the interval between the death of his master and the appearance of De Worde's first production was principally occupied in rearrangements and in pro-curing new type. In the colophon of Hilton's "Ladder of Perfection," printed in 1494, he notices the death of his master, and in the second verse mentions the patronage which he himself had re-

Bride, Fleet-street, before the high altar of St. Katharine. He may have lived, however, in a different house, as, in the colophon of a work printed in 1532, he is stated to be living "in flete-strete, at the sygne of the Sonne, agaynst the Con-dyth." The situation must have been somewhere about the present Ludgate-circus, where there was a conduit from Ludgate-hill to Fleet-street. "In this parish of St. Bridget," says Stow, "was a messuage or inn called the Falcon, in the tenure of the famous printer." It is supposed that Wynken de Worde died in 1534, although the colophon to his

edition of "Æsop" is dated 1535. Dibdin shows that his will was proved on January 19 of that year, however. It is not known whether he was married. According to the custom of his time, he was a stationer, since he calls himself in his will "citizen and stationer of London."

made use of. Some of these were said by Herbert "to be in use to this day." He also had a larger variety of sorts and sizes than his predecessors. It has been supposed by some that he was the first printer who introduced the Roman character into England, but it was his con-

He was also a member of the Leathersellers' Company.

Herbert says that, although De Worde was the immediate successor of Caxton, yet he improved the art to a very great degree of perfection. He cut a new set of punches, and cast the founts that he

temporary, Richard Pynson, who is entitled to the honour. Rowe Mores says that Wynken de Worde was his own typefounder; while Dibdin says that the type with which he printed most of his early folio volumes is not, to the best of his recollection, to be found in any of the books printed abroad at the same period. Mores further says that Wynken de Worde's Gothic type has " been the pattern for his successors in the art."

Devices.—Nine devices are known to have been used by Wynken de Worde.

1. The " white - grounded Caxton device," which is merely a copy of Caxton's smallest device. It was the first adopted by Wynken de Worde, being used by him only " at Westminster," or " Jn Caxton's house," without any other colophon.

2. The "small black-grounded Caxton device." It is an elongated variation of the preceding, without the border, surrounded by a narrow double line, and leaving the letters, cyphers, flourishes, and ornaments drawn in white upon a black stellated background. On a narrow white space beneath the device, which in No. 1 is filled with leaves and flowers, is the name of Wynken de Worde in small stout black letter. The present was one of the earliest devices used by this printer in Fleet-street.

3. A very rare tripartite device, nearly square, and enclosed by one strong black line. At the top is a scroll of three folds placed between two blazing stars, having upon it the name of Wynken de Worde in small stout black letters. Beneath the centre of the scroll is a crescent, supporting a star between its horns ; and below, occupying almost the whole breadth of the cut, are Caxton's initials and cypher, linked together by large and grotesque knots, all cut in outline. The bottom of this device displays the sun, standing between three tall flowers growing out of the ground on the left hand, and a vine with grapes on the right. A tuft of grass and leaves appears at the root of each plant, and another rises out of the bottom centre of the engraving next to the frame.

4. The "flowery Caxton device." A square device, rather smaller than the last, consisting of the "W.C." and cypher reversed, in strong black letters on a white ground ; while, from the centre beneath, spring out two branches with four flowers on each, inclining down on each side. The whole is within a narrow border of somewhat rich foliage, bounded both without and within by a double line, but that on the outside of all is considerably thicker than the rest. At each of the four angles of the border is a black square, containing a rose or star drawn upon it in white. Used only at Westminster.

5. The tripartite device. This, divided into three parts lengthways, is very interesting. The upper third alludes to the sign of Wynken de Worde's habitation in Fleet-street, the "Golden Sun," standing on a flat crescent. The middle refers to his connexion with Caxton, as it is occupied with the letters W.C. and the cypher. The lower refers to himself and his royal patroness, Margaret, mother of Henry VII., since he introduces his own name and the royal supporter, the greyhound. On the edge of the scroll is a rude representation of a sagittarius, lying down and holding up his bow with his left hand.

6. The common or largest tripartite device, which we reproduce. It is an upright parallelogram, surrounded and divided by double line. The contents of the divisions are nearly the same as in No. 5, but they are larger. The crescent in the upper one is omitted. The small stars are differently arranged. The initials in the centre are particularly large and handsome. In the lowest compartment the scroll has a double outline, and with the sagittarius and hound is reversed. Wynken de Worde used this device more frequently than any other, and is supposed to have adopted it about 1504.

7. The sagittarius device, in black, with white characters. Between two sagittarii is the device of Caxton ; above, the sun and flaming stars ; below, W.C. in Roman letters. Outside, the device at the foot, Wynken de Worde in black letters.

8. The picturesque device, copied from one belonging to Froben, with the omission of part of the background. It consists of a semicircular arch, supported by short pillars, with foliated capitals, plinths, and bases ; on the top of each is a boy habited like a soldier, with a spear and shield. Immediately within the arch is a sun with double rays ; on the left of which is an eight-pointed star, and on the right a crescent, with a three-quarter face in it. Round these, five small stars. Below, a large cartouche German shield supported by three boys. In the background, hills with two buildings. Upon the shield, a small black W.C. and cypher with an heraldic rose, &c. Beneath the engraving, "Wynken Worde." The whole surrounded by a double line. Supposed to have been adopted 1521. It was usual with De Worde to enlarge this device with four ornamental pieces of wood and metal, which formed a border, and which contained Caxton's cypher on a shield in the centre of the upper and lower pieces. These mov-

able decorations were also frequently used as an inclosure for his titles.

9. A large royal and heraldic device used as a frontispiece to acts of parliament, &c. The device is in the form of an upright parallelogram, surrounded by a double line. These enclose a species of arched panel, including clustered columns and Gothic mouldings. Under

An interesting account of this and the other devices is given in Johnson's "Typographia," vol. i. pp. 401-405.

The accepted "portrait" of De Worde, like that of Caxton, is entirely imaginary, and was first invented by W. Faithorne, jun. (*q.v.*). From the same book in the Harleian collection as that which contained the fictitious head of Caxton,

WORDE (WYNKYN DE).

the arch, two large shields, one on the left, with three fleurs-de-lys for France, the other bearing France and England quarterly ; each surmounted by a crown. Above the two shields, a demi-angel with expanded wings, an angel being the favourite supporter of Henry VII. Below portcullises, the Tudor emblem. At the bottom, a greyhound and dragon.

another purporting to be Wynken de Worde was engraved on wood for Ames. We reproduce this. After having for many years been received as genuine, it was discovered to be the portrait of Joachim Ringelberg, a scholar of Antwerp, the original being affixed to his "Elegantiæ" (Antwerp, 1529, 8vo.).—*See* Dibdin, "Decameron," vol. ii. p. 289.

YEATON (Charles C.). Manual of the Alden Type-setting and Distributing Machine: an Illustrated Exposition of its Mechanism, with Tabular Statements of the Weight of every Piece, including Estimates of Cost of Labour and Material; a Summary of the Amount of Type-setting annually executed; an Authentic Sketch of the History and Progress of the Invention, with a Proposed Plan of Future Operations for the Alden Type-setting and Distributing Machine Company. New York: 1865. Royal Folio. pp. 246. Profusely illustrated with mechanical engravings.

Only 100 copies printed. Unique as a specimen of curious tabular work and misdirected labour, for the machine was radically altered soon after the publication of the book. The 100 copies cost over $10,000.

———— A Letter to the Proprietors of the Alden Type-setting and Distributing Machine Company. Without place or date. New York: 1867. 8vo. pp. 64.

The complaint of Yeaton at his expulsion from the direction of the company for extravagant mismanagement.

TIMOTHY ALDEN, the inventor of the Alden Type-setting and Distributing Machine, was born at Yarmouth, Massachusetts, June 14, 1819, and died at New York, December 4, 1858. At the age of sixteen he learned the trade of a printer in Massachusetts, and continued at it till 1846. When only nineteen years of age, he announced his purpose of inventing a type-setting machine, and, although his project was ridiculed as visionary, he continued to devote his best thoughts and energies to its realisation. He removed to New York in 1846, and thenceforth applied himself sedulously to his favourite idea with such success, that a practical, though imperfect, machine was completed and patented in various countries in 1856. The English patent is No. 3089, December 29, 1856, "for setting and distributing printing types." By this time, incessant toil and mental anxiety had so pressed upon his spirits, that his vitality gave way, and his health rapidly declined till the day of his death.

A very large amount of money and labour was lavished upon this machine, but it was never made efficient. At a trial in 1865, in the office of the *New York Tribune*, it was proved that, although the machine could set as much type in one hour as could be done by five men in the same time, the cost of the composition so done was greater than that of hand-labour. The original machine both distributed and set up type, which was laid on a type-carrying wheel supported in a horizontal position above a suitable table of a horse-shoe form, around which the type cases were arranged. These cases consisted of a series of channels terminating near the circumference of the wheel. Keys actuated levers which brought the type to the setting-table (*see* "Abstracts of Specifications relating to Printing," vol. i. p. 570: and "American Encyclopædia of Printing," *s.v.* Alden, T. ; Alden Machine ; Type-setting Machines). At p. 478 is a view of the machine. The proprietors have practically abandoned the original machine, and made separate machines for composition and distribution.

YOUNG & MINNS. The Defence of Young & Minns, Printers to the State, before the Committee of the House of Representatives. With an appendix containing the debate. Boston, U.S.A. : 1805. 8vo.

ZACCARIA (Antonucci [Gaetano]). Catalogo ragionato di opere stampate per Fr. Marcolini da Forli, con memorie biografiche del medesimo Tipografo raccolte dall' Avv. Raffaele di Minicis, dissertazione. Fermo : 1850. 8vo. pp. 93.

——— Memorie biogr. int. al tipografo Fr. Marolini da Forli, con un catalogo rag. di opere stampate dal medes. Con appendice. 2 parts. Fermo : 1850-53. 8vo.

——— Catalogo di opere ebraiche, greche, latine ed italiane stampate dai celebri tipografi Soncini ne' secoli xv e xvi, accresciuto dal medesimo ora per cura di Cresc. Giannini corretto e migliorato. Come nella prima edizione ci sono premesse le breve notizie storiche degli stessi tipografi dettate dal Cav. Zefirino de Cesenate. Fermo : 1863. 8vo.

The Soncini family were the first printers at Soncini, near Cremorne, in Lombardy, where they set up a press for the production of Hebrew books in 1472 or 1473, the first book issued by them with a date being in 1484. Only 150 copies were printed of the above work.

——— Lettera sopra alcune giunte e correzioni le quali potrebbone farsi al libro del padre Orlandi, sull' origine e progressi della Stampa. [In Callogerà, raccolta di opuscoli.] pp. xlv. 213.

ZAENEKER (Joh. Dav.). Bey der doppelten Jubelfreude der edlen Buchdruckerkunst in Preussen, da selbige das dritte Jahrhundert der Erfindung, das Reussnerishe aber Dezcrote seines Ruhmes Feyerte. Königsberg : 1740. Folio. Single sheet.

ZAFFAUK (Josef).   Militair-Kartographie.   Vienna :   1873.   8vo.
pp. 38.

Report on the exhibits at the Vienna World's Exhibition in 1873, concerning the
production of geographical maps and military charts.

ZAINER (Gunther).   Etymologies of St. Isidore.   Augsburg
1472. 4to.

This work, previously referred to, was
the first printed with Roman letters in
Germany. Gunther Zainer, of Reutlingen,
who probably learned his art in the neigh-
bouring city of Strasbourg, appears to
have established the first press at Augsburg, and in 1468 printed a small folio,
entitled "Meditationes vitæ domini nostri
Jesu Christi," by Bonaventure. In 1469,
"La Somme de Jean de Ambach," and
an edition of the celebrated "Catholicon"
were issued. Zainer's books were all

printed in the semi-Roman character,
first used by the Cologne printers; but
in 1472 he introduced for the first time a
true Roman letter, in imitation of that
cast by Jenson, at Venice, and printed
with it the work cited above. Zainer
appears to have relinquished the art in
1475, and died in 1478, by which time
three other presses had been established
in Augsburg ; one by John Schüssler,
one by John Bämler, and a third at the
monastery of St. Ulric.

ZALUSKI (Jos.).   Programma litterarum ad bibliophilos, typothetas,
et bibliopegas, tum et quo suis liberalium artium amatores.
[Dantisci] : 1734.   4to.

ZAMBRINI (Francisco).   Le opere volgari à Stampa dei secolo xiii
e xiv, indicate e descritte.   4th edit. accomp. di tremila citazioni.
Bologna : 1878.   8vo.   pp. 565.   2 vols.

A second edition was issued in 1854.

ZANDER (C.).   Handbuch enthaltend das Reichgesetz über die
Presse vom 7 Mai 1874.   Leipzig : 1880.   8vo.

ZANETTI (A.).   Le premier siècle de la chalcographie, ou catalogue
des estampes du cabinet du Comte Cicognara.   Venice : 1837.
8vo.

See also CICOGNARA.

ZANI (Pietro).   Materiali per servire alla Storia dell' origine e de'
progressi dell' incisione in rame ed in legno, e sposizione della
scoperta d' una stampa originale del celebre Maso Finiguerra
fatta nel Gabinetto Nazionale de Parigi.   Parma : 1802. 8vo.

ZANTEDESCHI (Francesco).   Memorie della Elettrotipia, con 5 tavole
elettrotipiche.   Venice : 1841.   8vo.

ZAPATER (Justo) and JARENO (José Garcia Alcaraz).   Biblioteca
enciclopedica popular ilstrada.   Sect. 1, Artes y oficior.   Manual
de Litografia.   Madrid : 1880.   8vo.   pp. 222 and plates.

ZAPF (Georg Wilhelm).   Aelteste Buchdruckergeschichte Schwabens ;
oder Verzeichniss aller von Erfindung der Buchdruckerkunst bis
1500 in Ulm, Esslingen, Reutlingen, Memmingen, Stuttgart,
Tübingen, Urach, Blaubeuren und Constanz gedruckten Bücher,
mit litterarischen Anmerkungen.   Ulm : 1791.   8vo.   pp.
xliv. 272.

———— Aelteste Buchdruckergeschichte von Mainz, von derselben Erfindung bis auf das Jahr 1499; verfasst, herausgegeben und mit Anmerkungen erläutert von Georg Wilhelm Zapf. Ulm : 1790. 8vo. pp. xvi. An historical introduction of 46 pp., and the body of the work with register of 176 pp. ; plates.

———— Annales typographicæ Augustanæ ab ejus origine 1466 usque ad annum 1530. Accedit F. A. Veith diatribe de origine et incrementis artis typographicæ in urbe Augusta Vindelica. Edidit, notisque litterariis illustravit. Augustæ Vindelicorum : 1778. 4to.

This was republished in German, with copious additions, at Augsburg, in two parts. 1786. 4to.

———— Augsburgs Buchdruckergeschichte, nebst den Jahrbüchern derselben. Erster Theil Vom Jahre 1468 auf das Jahr 1500. Verfasset, herausgegeben und mit literarischen Anmerkungen. Augsburg : 1788. 4to. 8 plates. pp. lxiv. 220. Zweiter Theil : Vom Jahre 1501, bis auf das Jahr 1530. Mit Zusätzen und Verbesserungen zum 1. Theil. Augsburg : 1791. 4to. pp. xxiv. 263 and 15 ; index to both parts.

———— Bibliographische Nachschriften von einem lateinischen Psalter u. andere bibliogr. Seltenheiten aus dem 15. Jahrh. Augsburg 1800. 4to.

———— Catalogus Librorum rarissimorum, ab artes typographiæ untio ad annum 1499 excusorum et in Bibliotheca Zapfiana extantium. Papenheim : 1786. 8vo.

———— Ueber das eigentliche Jahr, in welchem die ehemalige berühmte Privatbuchdruckerei ad insigne Pinus in Augsburg ihren Anfang genommen. Vom Geheimrath Zapf. Augsburg : 1805. 8vo. pp. 32.

———— Ueber eine alte und höchst seltene Ausgabe von des Joannis de Turrecremata, explanatio in psalterium und einige typographische Seltenheiten. Eine litterarisch-bibliographische Abhandlung vom Geheimrath Zapf. Nürnberg : 1803. 4to.

———— Vorläufige Nachricht von der ehemaligen berühmten Privatbuchdruckerey ad insigne pinus in Augsburg, an Herrn Konrektor D. Johann Gottlob Lunze in Leipzig vom Geheimrath Zapf. Augsburg : 1804. 8vo. pp. 32.

An interesting tract on private printing-offices.

ZASII (U.). J. C. Friburg. quondam celeberrimi epistolæ ad viros ætatis suæ doctissimos. Quas partim ex autographis primum edidit, partim hinc atque illinc dispersas collegit, illustravit, et commentarium de illius vita præmisit J. A. Riegger. Ulmæ : 1774. 8vo.

Of particular importance on account of the history of printing in the town of Basle, and especially on account of the history of the family of Froben.

ZAUGHELLINI (Prof. Ab. Dott. Ant.).   Sulla Invenzione della Stampa. Milan: 1866. 4to.

ZECH (Josef Joh. Nep.).   Gott grüss die Kunst! Jahrbuch deutscher Buchdrucker für 1859. Agram: 1859. 4to. pp. vi. 88.
A collection of essays on printing or by printers, partly original, partly reprinted from the *Journal fur Buchdruckerkunst.*

ZEGGELEN (W. J. van).   Costerliedjes. Souvenir aan Haarlems julijfeesten in 1856. Haarlem: 1856. 12mo. and 16mo.

ZEISTRE (J. G.).   Von dem Nutzen und dénen Verdiensten der Buchdruckerkunst. Budessin 1740. 4to.

ZELL (K.).   Festrede zur iv. Säcularfeier der Erfindung der Buchdruckerkunst am 24. Janv. 1840 gehalten bei der Festversammlung im Rathhaussaale. Carlsruhe: 1840. 8vo. pp. 12.

——— Ueber Zeitungen der alten Römer. 2te Ausgabe. Heidelberg 1873. 8vo. pp. 248.

ZELL (Ulrich).—*See* "Cologne Chronicle."

This name, omitted by inadvertence from the review of the invention controversy *s. v.* KOSTER, *ante,* and from the excerpt from the "Cologne Chronicle" (*q.v.*), is important in typographical history, as that of the first printer at Cologne. He was an industrious printer there for more than forty years, but never printed a book in German, nor did he adopt any of the improvements of the printers of Italy. He adhered rigidly to the severe style of his master Schöffer, printing all his books from three sizes of a rude face of a round Gothic type. Madden supposes that he went to Cologne in 1462, and was engaged by the brotherhood of the Life-in-Common at Weidenbach, near that city, to assist them with his new art of printing in their pious task of making books. (*See* MADDEN, J.P.A., "Lettres d'un Bibliographe," 2nd series, No. 15, *ante,* and 1st Series, No. 5, *et passim.*) Zell's name appears for the first time in a book dated 1466, which date may be accepted as indicative of the time when he left the monastery and began to print on his own account.
Zell's name appears in the earliest notice of book-printing in the Netherlands, the "Cologne Chronicle" (*q.v.*) of 1499. The passage is translated in full in Hessel's Haarlem Legend (*see* HESSELS), pp. 7 and 8. "The origin and progress of the art was told me verbally by the honourable master Ulrich Zell, of Hanau, state printer at Cologne, anno 1499, and by whom the said art came to Cologne." Zell here relates not what he had seen, but what he had heard; he was either a mere child —or possibly was not born when Gutenberg began to experiment with types at Strasburg about 1436, or sixty-three years before this chronicle was printed. Zell's statement is the earliest acknowledgment of the priority of book-printing in Holland.
All the biographers of Caxton, previous to Mr. William Blades, speak of Ulric Zell as his preceptor in printing, and seem to believe that he supplied the English mercer with his first types. Van Praet, in 1829, showed that it was Colard Mansion, not Zell, with whom Caxton was associated abroad. Mr. Blades followed up the identification in his monograph of the English protoprinter, published in 1861.—*See* VAN PRAET and BLADES, W., *ante.*

ZELTNER (Gustav Georg).   Kurz-gefasste Historie der gedruckten Bibel-Version und anderer Schriften D. Mart. Lutheri, in der Beschreibung des Lebens und Fatorum Hanns Luffts, berühmten Buchdruckers und Händlers zu Wittenberg, auch anderer dasigen und benachbarten Typographorum. Nürnberg and Altdorff: 1727. 4to. pp. 114.

An account of the life and works of Lufft, printer and publisher of Nuremberg, who published Luther's Bible and other works of the great Reformer. Portraits of Lufft, Rhau, Gutenberg, Faust, Mentel, and Koster.

ZELTNER (J. C.). Correctorvm in typographiis ervditorvm centvria, speciminis loco collecta. Norimbergæ: 1716. 8vo. 600 engravings.

A work of considerable interest, containing the lives and labours of celebrated Press-readers. A second edition was issued in 1720, under the following title:—

———— Theatrum Virorum Eruditorum qui speciatim typographiis laudabilem operam præstiterunt. Norimbergæ: 1720. 12mo.

ZENGER (John Peter). Remarks on the Trial of John-Peter Zenger, of New York, Printer, who was lately try'd and acquitted for Printing and Publishing two Libels against the Government. With the Pleadings and Arguments on both sides. Printed for J. Wilford, behind the Chapter-house, St. Paul's Churchyard. London: 1738. 4to. pp. 32 besides the title-page.

The writer, who sides strongly with Zenger, signs himself at the end "Indo-Britannicus."

———— A Brief Narrative of the Case and Tryal of John Peter Zenger, Printer of the New York *Weekly Journal.* Boston: 1738. 4to. pp. 48.

JOHN PETER ZENGER began life as a printer at New York in 1726. In 1733 he started the second newspaper in that city, called the *Weekly Journal.* It soon assumed political importance from the unusual boldness with which the Government measures were attacked. In 1735 he was tried by commission for libel and acquitted, amidst the greatest excitement, the Advocate who defended him having the freedom of the city presented to him in a full Court of the Mayor, Aldermen, and Common Council. This was the first trial, in a question concerning the liberty of the Press, in which the principle since successfully maintained against the adverse ruling of the judges, that the jury is judge of the law as well as of the fact. The trial attracted great attention in England as well as America, and the report of it passed through several editions, of which may be noticed Boston and London, 1738, 4to. pp. 48, 1739, 1750, 1752 and 1791. New York, 1770, 4to.

———— The Case and Tryal of John Peter Zenger, of New York, Printer, who was lately tryed and acquitted for printing and publishing a libel against the Government, with the pleadings and arguments on both sides. London: 1750. 8vo.

Although dated in Boston, this tract was printed in London, by Thomas Fleet, at the Heart and Crown.

———— Another edition. London: 1750. 8vo.

ZENGHELLINI.—*See* BERNARDI, J.

ZENO (Apostolo). Notizie letterarie intorno ai Manuzi stampatori, ed alla loro famiglia. Venezia: 1736. 8vo.

A few copies re-printed from the "Epistole Famigliari."

VOL. III.   Q

ZEREN (Phil. von). Lobrede von der Buchdruckerkunst mit Anmerkungen, darinnen derselben Erfindung und Alterthum erörtert wird. Hamburg : 1642. 4to.

ZESTERMANN (A. C. A.). Die Unabhängigkeit der deutschen xylographischen Biblia Pauperum von der lateinischen xylographischen Biblia Pauperum nachgewiesen. Leipzig 1866. Folio. With one plate.

———— *See* WEIGEL and ZESTERMANN.

ZIEGLER (Frid.). De typographica arte declamat. in promotione publica Gymnasii Basileensis die 29. Mai ˙1827, recitandam composuit. Basileæ : 1827. 4to. pp. 6.

ZIJL. (W. C. van). Mijmering van het oude standbeeld van Laurens Janszoon Coster (Afgeluisterd). Ten voordeele van het feest der onthulling van diens standbeeld. Hilversum : 1856. 8vo.

ZIMMERMANN (Dr. Ed.). Die Reichsdruckerei gegenüber der Privat-Industrie. Berlin : 1880. 8vo. pp. 50.

ZINCKEN (C.). Schrift-Proben * * * wie solche zu Wittenberg in C. Zinckens Giesserey befindlich sind. 1743. 8vo.

ZUBRZYCKIEGO (D.). Historyczne Badania cdrukarniach Rusko. Slowianskich w Galicyi. Przez Dyonizego Zubrzyckiego-Lwow : 1836. 8vo. pp. 90 and 2 leaves.
An account of the first Press at Lemberg in Poland.

ZU dem glücklich erlebten dritten Jubelfest der vortrefflichen Buchdruckerkunst wünschte den Jenaischen Buchdrucker Herren und sämmtlichen Kunstverwandten ergebenst Glück derselben und der Kunst aufrichtiger Freund. Jena : 1740. Folio. pp. 8.

ZUM Andenken an das 400-jährige Jubiläum der Erfindung der Buchdruckerkunst am 24. Juni 1840. Bremen : 1840. Folio. 2 sheets.

ZUM Andenken an Friedrich Karl Heitz, Buchdrucker u. Buchhändler. Strassburg : 1867. 8vo. pp. 16.

ZUM Gedächtniss der IV Säcularfeier der Erfindung der Buchdruckerkunst in Heidelberg am 24. Juni 1840. Heidelberg : 1840. 8vo.

ZUNCKEL (Heinr. Gottfr.). In laudem Joannis Gutternbergii inventoris artis typographicae et ejus tertii Jubilaei. Regensburg : 1740. 4to.

ZUNZ (L.). Zur Geschichte und Literatur. 1 Vol. Berlin : 1845. 8vo. [pp. 354-59 : Drucker und Drucke von Mantua, 1476-1662.]

ZUR Arbeiter-Versicherung. Geschichte und Wirken des Unter-stützungs-Vereines deutscher Buchdrucker, 1866–82. Reudnitz : 1883. 2nd edition. 8vo.

ZUR Erinnerung an das fünfzigjährige Jubiläum der Firma F. A. Brockhaus in Leipzig am 13. u. 14. Juli 1856. Leipzig : 1857. 4to. Plates.

ZUR Feier des vierten Säcular-Jubelfestes der Buchdruckerkunst, welche im Saale der hiesigen Ressource am 24. Juni 1840 Vormittags 9 Uhr veranstaltet werden wird, ladet ergebenst ein die Oberlausitzische Gesellschaft der Wissenschaften. Inhalt : Beschreibung einer neuerfundenen Manier der Vervielfältigung bildlicher Gegenstände. Nebst einigen Proben. Görlitz. 4to.

The newly-invented method was called Gypsography by its inventor, the police-director Kohler, of Görlitz. He covered a piece of thin sheet-iron with a layer of gypsum, in which the figure to be re-produced was engraved with a needle, so as to lay open the iron of the sheet. The raised block to be printed from was produced by means of the stereotype process, but the results of the gypso-graphy were hardly anything but the rude experiments of an amateur.

ZUR frohen Feyer als J. Th. Edler von Trattner, 1802, die Stelle seiner Grossvaters als Druckherr antratt. Wien : 1802. Folio.

ZUR vierten Feier der Erfindung der Buchdruckerkunst. [In " Deutsche Vierteljahrschrift 1840, No. 2. Stuttgart.

ZUR IV Säcularfeier der Erfindung der Buchdruckerkunst. Dresden : 1840. Folio. pp. 6.

ZUR IV Säcularfeier der Erfindung der Buchdruckerkunst durch Johannes Gutenberg. Hamburg : 1840. 4to.

ZUREN (The Burgomaster van).—*See* VAN ZUREN.

ZÜRICH. Denkschrift der Museumsgesellschaft in Zürich. Zur Feier des 24. Junius 1840. 1840. 4to.

ZÜRICH. Geschichte und Statistik des Unterstützungs-Vereins für Buchdrucker u. Schriftgiesser in Zürich von 1819 bis 1869. Zürich 1869. 8vo.

ZUSAMMENSTELLUNG der wichtigsten in Württemberg geltenden Bestimmungen über Presssachen mit kurzen Erläuterungen. Von einem Rechtsgelehrten. Blaubeuren : 1864. 8vo.

THE END.

LONDON :

WYMAN AND SONS, ORIENTAL AND CLASSICAL PRINTERS,

GREAT QUEEN STREET, W.C.